GW01340149

PORSCHE

Shotaro Kobayashi

Motorbooks International
Publishers & Wholesalers Inc.

ISBN
0-87938-001-2
Library of Congress Catalog Card Number
75-181085

© **Motorbooks International Publishers & Wholesalers Inc.**
1973

All rights reserved. No part of this publication may be reproduced without prior written permission from the publisher.

Motorbooks International Publishers & Wholesalers Inc., 3501 Hennepin Avenue South, Minneapolis, Minnesota 55408, U.S.A.

Translated from Japanese. Printed in Japan.

Motorbooks Library
Marque Series

Contents

Foreword	Porsche—An Engineering Victory.	5
Chapter 1	The History Prior to the Porsche: From the First Electric Car to the Volkswagen.	7
Chapter 2	The 356 Series.	23
Chapter 3	The Early Carrera and Renn Sport (1953 to 1963).	56
Chapter 4	GP Formula Car (1957 to 1962).	76
Chapter 5	The 911/912 and 914.	81
Chapter 6	Racing Models Since the 904.	103

Photograph Credits

James A. Allington
81

Anglia Art
136

Pete Biro
137

Bernard Cahier
104, 125, 131

Daimler-Benz AG
9-11

Eric della Faille
89, 113, 115, 118, 121, 122, 132

Theo Page
111

David Phipps
90, 91, 99, 101, 116, 117, 119, 120, 134

Dr. Ing. h.c.F. Porsche KG
1-8, 12-37, 39-80, 82-88, 98, 103, 105-109, 126-130, 133, 135

FOREWORD
Porsche — An Engineering Victory

Dr. Ferdinand Porsche (1875—1951)

In the world of automotive industry today, giant international enterprises are fighting fiercely for survival, using as their only weapon sales power coupled with low cost based on mass production. In striking contrast to them is the Porsche Company, which specializes in the manufacture of expensive sports cars well known for their high quality and marked individuality. With limited capital and relatively small production, it is firmly maintaining its integrity as an enterprise. Admitting its close relationship with the Volkswagen Company with its huge capital, the uniqueness of Porsche's successful management is scarcely marred by the latter's existence. Its success is, in short, a sheer victory of engineering — a sharp rebuttal to those who believe that the fate of an enterprise depends entirely on its sales power.

It was back in 1949, when European countries were at last emerging from the postwar chaos, that a small, silver-colored sports coupé named for Dr. Ferdinand Porsche made its debut at the annual show in Geneva. In the first fiscal production year of 1950, the Porsche Company had less than a hundred men on its staff and turned out only 410 cars. Even in those early years, almost half of its staff designers were working at the request of outside firms on various devices including the famous Porsche method of synchromesh; and already the Porsche Company was an enterprise that maintained itself not only by the manufacture of sports cars, but also by its engineering skill and patents. Even today Porsche produces only about 1,500 cars a month and ranks among medium and small-scale enterprises. To motor sport enthusiasts and sports car lovers, however, the name "Porsche" brings a feeling akin to reverence.

Since the Le Mans race of 1951, Porsche has been practically the only manufacturer consistently participating in various events of international racing. Its tireless efforts and technical achieve-

Ferry Porsche, eldest son of Dr. Porsche

ed as ever by strong individuality. But that person would be ignorant of the human side of their manufacturer. Even today the company is run very much like a "family" business (in the best sense of the word) of the Porsche family.

The death of Dr. Ferdinand Porsche on January 30, 1951, put an end to his great and colorful career. But his eldest son Ferry, who was already a distinguished designer, immediately took over the difficult task of managing the company. Together with Karl Rabe, who had long been a right-hand man to his father, Ferry promoted the development of the sports car type 356.

Ferry's four sons have all reached manhood and now hold responsible positions in various departments of the Porsche Company. Worthy of special mention is Ferdinand III (affectionately called "Butzi"), whose superior ability as style designer was early recognized with his body styling of the 911 and the 914. Dr. Porsche's daughter, Louise, married Dr. Piëch, who had been a collaborator of her father during the early years of the Porsche Company. A son from this union has become an able designer and was put in charge of the development of the racing car model 906 and a series of models following it. In addition to Karl Rabe, mentioned above, there are a number of men who have been on the staff of the company since 1930, when Dr. Porsche opened his design office. They include: Kales, formerly of Skoda, who is an expert on the air-cooled engine; Kommenda, who came from Daimler-Benz and now specializes in body designing; and Mickl, a mathematician. The founder's ideals and traditions are still positively alive in the Porsche Works.

ments were amply rewarded when it won the manufacturer's championship three years in succession. This record feat began in 1968 and culminated in 1970, when the company gained an overwhelming victory at Le Mans.

In these modern days when automobile design is made by committees with the aid of computers, it is said that there is little possibility of an individual designer's ideas taking form in a concrete design. One may well wonder, therefore, why the Porsche cars of today are mark-

Ferdinand Porsche III, grandson of Dr. Porsche

CHAPTER 1
The History Prior to the Porsche: From the First Electric Car to the Volkswagen

It is true that the Volkswagen and the Porsche are among the most important works of Dr. Porsche; but, needless to say, these products did not just appear all of a sudden. In order to discuss the Porsche of today, we must first trace its history.

When Dr. Porsche designed the prototype Volkswagen sometime between 1931 and 1936, he was already in his late fifties. This means that the Volkswagen was a product of the last stage of his forty-year career as an engineer. Its design was based on the knowledge and experience he had accumulated in his long career, which was devoted entirely to designing: from grand-prix racing cars to military tractors — from the V-16 cylinder racing engine to agricultural diesel engines.

Looking back to those early years following World War II, we cannot help feeling it strange that the Volkswagen, a car of such unorthodox design, should surpass the Model T Ford in long-run sales all over the world. The air-cooled rear engine, the beetle-like style designed solely for function, the body welded to the backbone-chassis which did not promise high productivity — everything about the vehicle was radically different from all others of that era. What prompted production of the Volkswagen was the fact that Hitler (the century's demagogue), with his political ambitions, urgently needed it as the most effective bait to win the favor of his people. Here, incidentally, we see an interesting example of historic coincidence.

The Volkswagen was certainly a people's car, intended for practical use and designed for production at a set cost. The engineering precision of its air-cooled, horizontally opposed 4-cylinder engine (whose power output, with great stress on engine durability, was intentionally held down by reducing the air intake) was unbelievably high for such a low-priced vehicle. Its independent front suspension, which was based on horizontal torsion bars and double trailing links, was identical to that used in the grand-prix racer that Dr. Porsche designed for Auto Union in the years between 1934 and 1937. As for its "aerodynamic" body (so called by the standard of that era), we are tempted to allude to the fact that when Dr. Porsche designed an experimental car with a 3.25-liter 8-cylinder engine for the Wanderer company in 1932, he placed on it a futuristic body which he had created using Dr. Kamm's aerodynamic theory.

Strange to say, Dr. Porsche was not a so-called "manufacturer" of automobiles. It was not until 1949, only two years before his death, that he founded a modest workshop of his own in order to produce the Porsche 356. This was his first attempt to be a manufacturer. Up to that time he had not been at all interested in producing and selling cars for his own sake. He was a designer to the core. True to his creed as a technician, he directed his undying enthusiasm toward the designing of the best

7

cars possible. His stubborn, uncompromising nature often brought him into conflict with managers who could not understand him. Moreover, the political vicissitudes in central Europe at that time obliged him to drift from one workshop to another.

Dr. Ferdinand Porsche was born in 1875, in Maffersdorf, Bohemia (at that time a part of Austria), as the second son of a metal worker. When he finished schooling at 16, his greatest interest was in automobiles and electricity, which had just reached the practical stage. He went to Vienna and became an apprentice at the Bela-Egger Electrical Company. In order to absorb necessary basic technical knowledge, he attended night classes at the Engineering Department of Vienna University. As this fact shows, he was practically a self-educated man. It was natural, therefore, that he was extremely pleased when he later received an honorary doctorate from the Technical University in Vienna, in recognition of his superior designs of aircraft engines and military vehicles made during his Austro-Daimler Company days.

During his apprenticeship at the Bela-Egger Company, the company's plant, one day, received a Lohner electric automobile for repair. Five weeks later young Porsche was employed by the Lohner Company, and this was the beginning of his life with automobiles. In 1900, Porsche exhibited his first design, the Lohner-Porsche Electrical Car, at the Paris Salon. This was an epoch-making vehicle. The complicated transmission was completely eliminated, and electric motors powered by batteries were built into the hubs of the two front wheels. His next step was to replace the heavy batteries with a gasoline engine; and then to couple a dynamo to the engine. Actually, the hybrid engine, which is now coming back into the limelight, was created by Dr. Porsche seventy years ago. Later, in 1906, when he became the chief designer at Austro-

Lohner-Porsche electric car, 1900
This was the first car designed by Dr. Porsche.

Lohner-Porsche electric racing car

Austro-Daimler 27/80 HP, 1910

Austro-Daimler "Sascha," 1922
This car had a 4-cylinder SOHC 1,100-cc engine and was fitted with four-wheel brakes.

Austro-Daimler ADV, 1921–1923

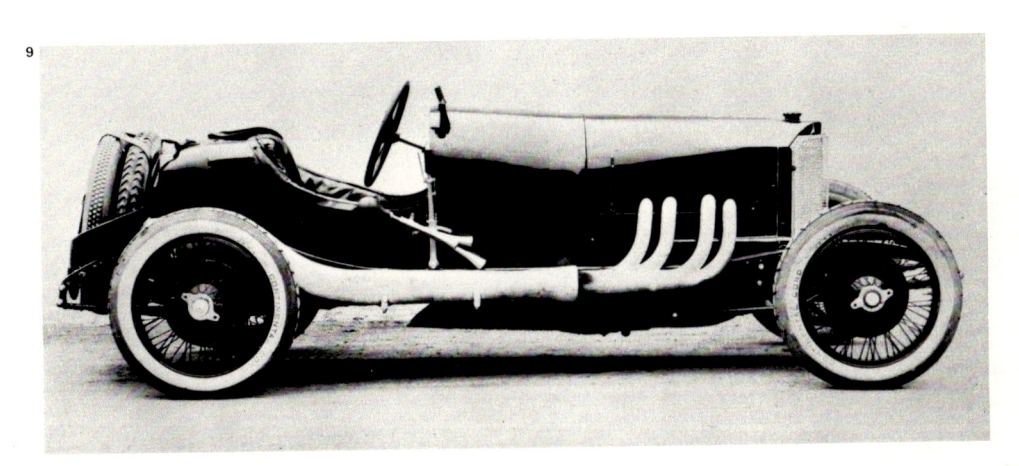

Mercedes 2-liter racing car, 1923–1924
It can be said that the status of Mercedes racing cars was greatly improved by Dr. Porsche.

Mercedes-Benz 38/250 SSK, one of the masterworks in classic sports car design

Daimler (then the largest automobile manufacturer in the Austro-Hungarian Empire), he had for the first time an opportunity to design a sports car from its beginning. This car was the 28/30 HP "Maja", a high-performance vehicle with a 4-cylinder SOHC 5.7-liter engine of advanced design. At the Prince Henry Trial held in the same year, the Maja captured the first, second, and third places. The man at the steering wheel of the victorious car was Porsche himself.

Porsche then made a number of improvements on the Maja. In the race held the following year, this new type, equipped with a smaller and lighter 27/80 HP engine and with an aerodynamic body having a tulip-shaped cross section, again won the first three places. As a result of these two successive victories, Porsche, as a designer-driver, suddenly became famous. What pleased him the most, however, was the opportunity to form close friendships with the top designers of those days, such as Vincenzo Lancia, Ettore Bugatti, Laurence Pomeroy (of the Vauxhall 30/98), Hans Ledwinka (of the Tatra); and to have technical discussions, his favorite avocation, with them to his heart's content. With Ledwinka, especially, he enjoyed a lifelong friendship. It is said that Ledwinka's air-cooled Tatra engine suggested many points to Porsche, and that the latter's swing axle, in its turn, greatly influenced the Tatra. Among important works left by Porsche during his Austro-Daimler days were various types of aircraft engines. The first aircraft engine designed by him was a water-cooled 4-cylinder OHV engine. To keep its weight down, the cylinder jacket was built of a thin steel plate welded around each of the cylinder

Mercedes-Benz 38/250 SS/SSK engine
Dr. Porsche was of the opinion that engines should also look fine externally.

barrels. Porsche used this method, without any change, in the supercharged sports car engine which he designed at Daimler—Benz after World War I. Even after he left the company, this method remained a traditional one for designing aircraft and racing car engines. (It was applied to the famous DB 601 fuel injection V-12 engine, the Mercedes W-196 engine of 1954, and even the 300 SLR Vertical 8-cylinder engine.)

After 1912, Porsche switched to designing air-cooled engines. His first air-cooled aircraft engine, a horizontally opposed 4-cylinder OHV engine, was such an outstanding work of that period that even the Beardmore Company of England took steps to manufacture it. Today, seeing an engine of this type exhibited in the Science Museum in England, we wonder at its close resemblance to the Volkswagen engine that came out later.

After her defeat in World War I, the Austro-Hungarian Empire was broken up and suffered dire poverty. It was Porsche's belief then that what Austria would need would be small cars, inexpensive to buy and maintain. But the management would not listen to his repeated proposals to this effect. About that time Citroen of France had already adopted the American system of mass-production and had started to turn out the Type 10-CV at the rate of 10,000 units per year. And in England, Lord Austin had completed the test-manufacture of the famous "Seven." At Austro-Daimler, however, managers with outmoded ideas, still immersed in the dreams of past years, clung to large luxury cars. The ADV, which appeared in 1921, was a luxury car with a 6-cylinder 4.4-liter SOHC engine. Both its sharp-pointed, V-shaped radiator and its steering gearbox were attached to the engine crankcase. The cylinder block was made of silumin alloy, and the rear axle case was also of light alloy casting. From a technical point of view, both the ADV and the smaller and more sporty ADM-I (2,540 cc) were excellent cars. But their sales potential was small, and the fortunes of the Austro-Daimler Company gradually declined.

Though uninterested in business matters, Porsche, as a technician, saw bright prospects for small cars and wished to realize his dream. Help came to him from an unexpected quarter—in the person of Count Sascha Kolowrat, a friend of Porsche and the owner of a film company in Austria. An enthusiastic motorist, the Count sympathized with Porsche's idea of a small, high-performance car and offered to defray all expenses for its research and test-manufacture.

Four small experimental sports cars were then built; and in appreciation of the financier, Porsche named them "Sascha." They were each equipped with a 4-cylinder OHC 1,100-cc (63 x 75 mm) engine and developed 45 horsepower. In 1922 the four Saschas participated in the Targa Florio, one of them driven by the Count himself and the others by company drivers. Unfortunately the car driven by the Count overheated its engine and was forced to retire from the race. But two others that took part in the 1,100-cc class event captured the first and second places; and the fourth car, which challenged the class for 2 liters and above, managed to win seventh place with an average speed of 35 mph. Its driver was Alfred Neubauer, who was unknown at that time. In that year alone, Saschas took part in 51 races, winning 43 first places and 8 second places; and as a result, the names of Porsche and Austro-Daimler resounded throughout Europe.

Porsche went further to test-manufacture 2-liter and 3-liter cars and was preparing to put them into production, when the management suddenly came out with an imprudent decision to stop participating in all racing activities. What had led to this decision was that unfortunate incident at Monza: the Sascha that took part in the Italian Grand Prix there crashed, owing to defective material of the wire wheels, and the driver was killed. When the management put all blame on Porsche, as the designer of the car, and banned further participation in 'dangerous' racing, he became angry. On the same day he tendered his resignation and left the Austro-Daimler Company.

In April, 1923, Porsche, at the age of 47, was welcomed into the Daimler Motoren A.G. in Germany as their chief designer. He brought along from Austro-Daimler, O. Koehler, his right-hand man, and Neubauer, a test driver.

Porsche's first work was the development of the 2-liter supercharged racing car which had been left behind, unfinished, by his predecessor, P. Daimler. Porsche improved the Roots-type supercharger by increasing its reliability, and the chassis by fitting front wheel brakes, among other things. The 4-cylinder OHC 2-liter engine had an output of 120 HP/4,500 rpm. In the Targa Florio of 1924 this car won the first, tenth, and fifteenth places with an average speed of 40 mph. This victory was regarded highly, not only in the sports world but also in academic circles, and the Technical College of Stuttgart awarded an honorary doctorate to Porsche as the designer of the car.

Porsche, it appears, believed that superchargers would be necessary in the future not only in racing cars but even in sports cars and high-performance utility cars. In 1924 he designed two types of cars, both of which had a supercharged 6-cylinder OHC engine. One was a 4-liter 15/70/100 HP, and the other a 6-liter 24/100/140 HP. These two types became the basis for the *Mercedes-Benz supercharged high-performance luxury vehicle, which was ultimately to develop into the SSKL. (*In 1926 the Daimler Company merged with the Benz Company and changed the car name to "Mercedes-Benz.") Both types had a 6-cylinder SOHC engine, whose cylinder block was of a light alloy and contained cast iron liners. The

Roots-type blower was driven vertically from the crankshaft end by means of bevel gears, and was put into operation when the throttle was opened fully. In 1926 the "K" Wagen, a 6,245-cc supercharged 33/180 K model, made its appearance. The Model 36/220 of 1927 was a large, luxurious sports car, whose chassis was the same as that of the Model 33/180 K, except that it was made lower. Though it was a large car with a 134-inch wheelbase and weighed over two tons, it had a speed of 108 mph. In 1928 an improved model, the 38/250 SS (7,069-cc 225 HP/3,200 rpm), appeared and then developed into the SSK model, which had a more powerful engine mounted on a shorter chassis. One might call this period the golden age of the Mercedes.

The Mercedes S series, which is counted among Dr. Porsche's masterworks, scored many successes in automobile races. They are too numerous to mention, but some of the notable victories were: first three places in the Grand Prix of Germany of 1927; first place by the SSK, driven by the famous Caracciola, and second and third places by the SS in the German G.P. of 1929; first place in the Mille Miglia of 1931, with an average speed of 62 mph; second place behind an Alfa in the Le Mans of the same year.

In October, 1928, Dr. Porsche left the Daimler-Benz Company owing to disagreements with the management of the company. As in the case of Austro-Daimler, the management was quite indifferent to his repeated proposals about his plans for small passenger cars. Up to that time, while striving to develop the 38/250 SS of the "super-dreadnought" class, Dr. Porsche had been carrying on the designing of a small, lightweight car, his long-cherished dream. By 1927 he had completed a 4-cylinder 1-liter test model. The test results of this car were very promising, but the management had absolutely no understanding of small cars and ordered Dr. Porsche to stop further work on his plan.

Immediately after leaving Daimler-Benz, Dr. Porsche received two offers, one from Tatra of Czechoslovakia and the other from Steyr of Austria. He chose the latter and became the chief designer for Steyr in January, 1929. In less than ten weeks Porsche completed the design of a 2-liter 6-cylinder "30" model. This model, with some improvements, was produced until about 1935 and became the mainstay of the Steyr Company.

Porsche next designed an 8-cylinder OHV 5.3-liter 100 HP car, a large vehicle christened Steyr "Austria." Personally driving this car, an elegant cabriolet, Porsche went to the Paris Salon of 1929. Year after year he attended this automobile show in Paris with great pleasure; for there he could not only inspect new models from various manufacturers, but also renew his acquaintance with many old designer friends from other countries and enjoy carrying on technical discussions with them far into the night.

The Austria won great popularity at the Paris Salon, as it was already equipped with an overdrive and a powerful servo-

Professor Porsche with a Wanderer 2-liter Cabriolet (Porsche Type 7), 1932, first product of the new Porsche firm. Ferry Porsche is inside the car.

brake system, well in advance of the trend. But misfortune was again waiting for Porsche. The Steyr Company, whose prosperity had been declining for some time, was now on the verge of bankruptcy and was eventually absorbed into the Austro-Daimler Company. Porsche found it against his conscience to work again for the very people with whom he had had such a violent clash of opinions some years before, and he resolutely tendered his resignation to Steyr.

In the fall of 1930, together with a few close friends, Dr. Porsche founded an independent design office at Kronenstrasse 14, Stuttgart. It was announced that this office, called "Dr. ing. h.c. Ferdinand Porsche GmbH." (Honorary Doctor of Engineering Ferdinand Porsche & Co., Ltd.), should be to design and test-manufacture automobiles, aircraft, and ships. The staff consisted of the following members: Karl Rabe (his assistant since Austro-Daimler days), Fröhlich and Zahradnik (both formerly of Steyr), Joseph Kales (An expert on air-cooled engines and formerly of Skoda), Kommenda (a body designer and formerly of Daimler-Benz), Mickl (a mathematician), and a few others. These staff members had all worked together with Porsche for many years and were thoroughly acquainted with the way of doing things peculiar to him. The youngest member was 21-year-old Ferry, Porsche's eldest son, who had just finished his apprenticeship at the Robert Bosch Company.

The first work of the office, an order placed by Wanderer, was to design a 2-liter medium size car. This was an advanced vehicle having a 6-cylinder 1.8-liter OHV engine with cast iron wet liners in a light alloy block. Its rear wheel suspension involved a swing axle and a lateral leaf spring. In the Porsche office they decided to number their designs consecutively and to give this Wanderer car the design number 7, or Type 7. (This car was not called Type 1 because Porsche, though not usual for him, thought it unwise to cause possible apprehension to his clients.)

Satisfied with the success of Type 7, Wanderer next ordered the design of a larger high-performance car. The result was the Type 8, test-manufactured in 1932, equipped with an 8-cylinder OHV

13

Wanderer 3.25-liter prototype (Porsche Type 8), 1932
This prototype was the only one built, and long served as Dr. Porsche's personal car.

14

Zündapp Prototype (Porsche Type 12), 1932
This prototype had a water-cooled 5-cylinder radial engine in the rear.

15 NSU "Volksauto" (Porsche Type 32), 1933
First design with air cooled flat-four engine.

16 Volkswagen-Series (Porsche Type 60), 1935 – 1936
About 50,000 units of this car were to be produced annually and to be sold at 990 marks (about $400.00) but because of the war, the plan was switched over to a model for military use.

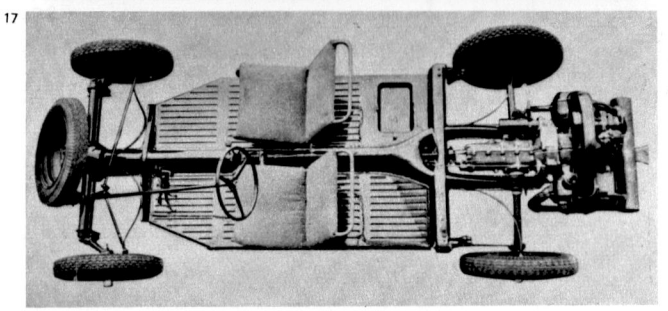

17 Chassis of the above car
The backbone platform, independent suspensions based on transverse torsion bars concealed in tubes, etc. show that this car was basically the same as postwar Volkswagens.

Several units of this record car were built for participation in the Berlin-Rome record run and attained a record speed of 90 MPH during test runs but, because of the war, this event was cancelled.

supercharged 3.25-liter engine and a very futuristic, streamlined body built by the Reutter Company. This body design was based on the so-called "Kamm's streamline theory" — a theory which Dr. Kamm of Stuttgart University had developed by wind-tunnel tests. A novel method in those days, it greatly influenced the small, lightweight Porsche cars which followed this Type 8 and prepared the way for the Volkswagen.

From 1931 onward, without interference from anyone, Porsche was able to carry out his long-cherished desire to create a small, lightweight passenger car. This project for the small car, named Type 12, encountered many problems but finally resulted in the birth of the Volkswagen. A prototype Volkswagen was finally completed in 1937. Its basic features (the air-cooled rear engine, the backbone-chassis, the beetle-shaped body welded integrally onto the chassis, the independent suspension based on the front and rear torsion bars) could already be noted, it is said, in the plan for the Type 12.

Ever-active Porsche, while working on the small-car project, created the design of an epoch-making grand-prix car. The Grand Prix races of 1932 to 1937 were held under a new formula, according to which the maximum weight of the car excluding oil, water, and tires was to be 750 kilograms, but within this weight limit any kind of engine was permitted. For a designer like Dr. Porsche this formula was indeed fascinating. His plan called for an engine so novel that it had not been advocated before: a V-16 cylinder SOHC 4.4-liter supercharged engine, with an output of at least 280 HP/5,000 rpm. This engine was placed at the rear of a very simple tube frame, but in front of the rear axle, and drove the rear wheels through a 5-speed transmission. There already existed a mid-engine grand-prix car — i.e. the Troppen Wagen designed by Dr. Rumpler for Benz in 1923 — but the honor of establishing the first great success in actual competition should go to this car of Dr. Porsche (called the "P-Wagen" at his office).

It was just about this time that four medium-size manufacturers in Germany — DKW, Audi, Horch, and Wanderer — merged together to form the Auto-Union. Porsche approached this new company and disclosed his plan for the above-mentioned racing car. Auto-Union, however, did not yet have the financial power to test-manufacture and develop the entirely new grand-prix racer and organize a racing team to enter international racing. The sudden appearance of Hitler on the scene changed the situation, and Dr. Porsche's P-Wagen rapidly materialized.

On January 30, 1933, Hitler was appointed chancellor, and history took a new turn. So far as Porsche was concerned, Hitler's rise to the top of political power was quite an unexpected stroke of luck; for, besides commanding the test-manufacture of the Volkswagen, Hitler, in order to show Germany's national prestige through automobile racing, promised to give subsidies to both Auto-Union and Mercedes for the manufacture of grand-prix racers. The cars manufactured thereby were the famous series of V-16 Auto-Unions which competed vigorously with Mercedes (equipped with an engine based on the 3-liter DOHC 8-cylinder engine that Dr. Porsche had designed while at Daimler-Benz) in the 750-kg formula races of 1934 to 1937. These Auto-Union cars, together with the Mercedes, made clean sweeps of the Grand Prix racing world. The V-16 Auto-Union Type A made its debut in 1934 with a 4.36-liter 295 HP/4,500 rpm engine. The following year this car was improved and became the Type B, with a more powerful 4.95-liter 375 HP/4,700 rpm engine, and with a remodeled rear suspension consisting of swing axles and torsion bars that passed through the side frame. This Type B developed a top speed of 180 mph. The 1936—1937 season saw the Type C with a 6,008-cc 520 HP/5,000 rpm engine, and with a maximum speed of over 186 mph.

Besides winning many races, the Auto-Union, with a specially designed aerodynamic body, broke many world speed records in 1937, on an autobahn sector in the outskirts of Frankfurt, with Rosemeyer at the wheel. Among these was one of 25.96 seconds for the standing start mile, which stood unbroken until 1959. Many innovative designs incorporated into this Auto-Union grand-prix car had great influence on subsequent car designing, not only for Porsche himself but also for other designers the world over. The numerous successes of the Auto-Union confirmed, favorably or unfavorably, the influence on maneuverability of the mid-engine layout (with large, heavy masses such as the engine, driver, and fuel tanks placed close to the center of gravity) and made Dr. Porsche a firm believer in the rear-engine and

Auto-Union Type C G.P. machine, 1936

Auto-Union V 16-cylinder engine, 1936-1937

21 Auto-Union G.P. record car, 1937, with a 6.3-liter 545 HP engine and a light, streamlined body
This photograph, taken in 1937, shows the car getting a pushstart.

22 Cisitalia 1.5-liter G.P. machine (Porsche Type 360), 1947–1949

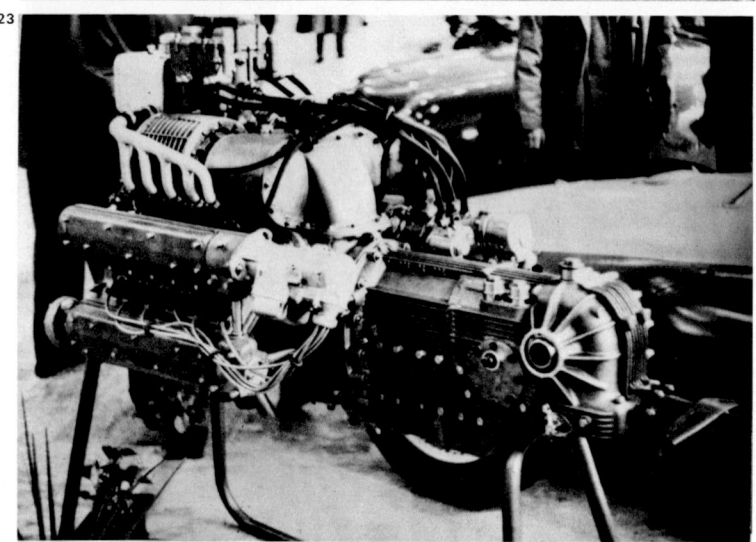

23 Engine of the above car: DOHC horizontally opposed, 12-cylinder, 1,498 cc. This engine, with a ZF 5 speed transmission, was very compact.

mid-engine arrangements. Here we find the cause of the growth in popularity of the Porsche in the postwar years.

Moreover, the independent front suspension based on a torsion bar and a double trailing link gave not a small shock to passenger car manufacturers in Europe. Many of them either purchased Porsche's patents or contracted directly with him for designing. Among them were Alfa-Romeo, Citroen, Vauxhall, and Morris. Alec Issigonis, who was then with Morris, was so impressed that he built a 750-cc sprint car ("Lightweight Special") by scaling down and simplifying the chassis of the previously mentioned Auto-Union.

For the period beginning a few years before and ending during World War II, Dr. Porsche was engaged in surprisingly diverse areas of designing activity. Among his designs were an electric generator rotated by a wind-driven propeller, a stationary Volkswagen engine for use with searchlights, a bus with an underfloor 5-cylinder radial engine, a new rubber suspension, and a 3-seater (three abreast with the driver in the middle) sports car with a V-16 P-Wagen engine placed in a midship position. Worthy of special mention may be the high-speed car T-80, which was intended to attain 435 mph in a trial to have been held in 1940. This trial was also a kind of political stunt that Hitler liked. He had planned to win back those world speed records which were all then held by British drivers such as George Eyston, John Cobb, and Sir Malcolm Campbell. The designing of this record car was delegated to Porsche, and the construction to Daimler-Benz. The car had a DB 601 V-12 aircraft engine located midship on a chassis with six wheels (the four rear wheels of which were driven), and the body even had horizontal fins to prevent lifting at high speed. In other words, the car already had the features of modern high-speed car designs. But this plan never bore fruit because of the Nazi invasion of Poland.

Besides this, there already existed, in 1938, a plan for a sports car based on the Volkswagen. To participate in the Berlin-Rome record run scheduled for June of the same year, Dr. Porsche built a car with a streamlined single-seater body placed on a prototype Volkswagen. With this car he succeeded in attaining a record speed of 90 mph, but again because of the war this project did not materialize.

With Germany's defeat in the war, Porsche was detained by the Allied Army. A born freedom-lover, he was of course against the political ideologies of the Nazis, but still it was undeniable that he had been in very close contact with Hitler and some of his staff, and that his technical skills had greatly contributed to the war power of Axis countries. Having fallen into the hands of the French, he was confined to a barracks used by the caretakers in the former residence of Louis Renault in Paris. During this time he was coerced into giving his opinions regarding the rear axle of the car which was to become the Renault 4 CV. After that, for about two years, until August, 1947, he was imprisoned in France and his property was confiscated. To help Dr. Porsche regain his freedom, Ferry Porsche and Karl Rabe, both of whom had already been freed, made tireless efforts. It is said that it was for the purpose of raising money to buy Dr. Porsche's freedom that they designed for Cisitalia of Italy a flat-12, 1.5-liter 4-wheel-drive grand-prix car.

Dr. Porsche, then over seventy, was in declining health. And when finally freed in August, 1947, after two years of imprisonment, he was a semi-invalid. How much Dr. Porsche contributed to the design of the Porsche 356 is not mentioned clearly in the formal record of the Porsche Company. The view generally held today is that since the 356 prototype was built between 1947 and 1948, it must have been Ferry

On June 3, 1950, fifty Type 356 cars and their owners gathered together from all over Europe to celebrate Dr. Porsche's 75th birthday

Porsche and Karl Rabe who designed it, and that the aged Porsche helped them by giving suggestions regarding details.

For Dr. Porsche, June 3, 1950 must have been an unforgettable date, for on that day a small party was held to honor old Ferdinand, who celebrated his 75th birthday at his home in a suburb of Stuttgart. Those present were his son, Ferry, and his design staff, some of whom had shared the joys and sorrows together with Ferdinand for as long as fifty years. Also present were Porsche owners who had come from all over Europe especially for this occasion. Old Ferdinand slowly walked among the fifty Porsche 356 cars assembled there, his face radiant with the deep joy and pride of an engineer who had devoted his whole life to designing automobiles. On January 30, 1951, Porsche passed away, closing his eventful and illustrious career.

CHAPTER 2
The 356 Series

Significance of the Porsche 356

The Porsche 356, which made its debut at the Geneva Show in the spring of 1948, was nothing but a "souped-up" Volkswagen; literally hand-built at Porsche's modest, temporary workshop in the little village of Gmünd, in Austria. This car was the first of the 356 series. Until the appearance of the entirely new 911, seventeen years later, the production 356 underwent constant research and improvement, and made the name of Porsche synonymous with small, high-performance GT cars. Today no one doubts the superior road-holding and reliability of the Porsche. At the time of its debut, however, its basic layout was so unorthodox and its maneuverability so inadequate, that to a certain extent it was inevitable that the car be criticized as "a Volkswagen overdosed with vitamins." Accordingly, public estimation of it was clearly divided.

Those drivers who were accustomed to the strong understeer of conventional front-engine sports cars, such as the MG and the Triumph TR-2, were alarmed at the sharp oversteer on early models of the Porsche and were liable to criticize unjustly that the Porsche became uncontrollable during cornering. Other drivers with more nerve (most of whom were Volkswagen drivers) were, from the beginning, wildly enthusiastic about this completely new sports car. Sports car lovers of the 1950's were clearly divided into pro- and anti-Porsche camps — actually many in the latter camp were simply prejudiced against the Porsche — and arguments between the two camps continue to this day.

The Porsche 356 was an outstanding product, and it added a new page to the history of sports cars. Before its appearance the main current of small sports cars was that of the vintage cars of England. A typical small sports car of those days had a ladder-type frame of low rigidity, hard suspension, a front engine which drove the fixed rear axle, and the extremely poor quality of the car's overall weather protection was taken for granted. Its acceleration was dependent on low gearing and, though adquate for short-distance sprinting, the car was not suited for long-distance touring. On good road surfaces the car, in exchange for hard riding, showed good maneuverability (which meant strong understeer). During cornering on bad surfaces, however, it had virtually no road-holding and required desperate struggles with heavy steering. Such were the standard characteristics of sports cars of those days.

The Porsche 356 completely broke down such fixed concepts of sports cars. The design objective consistently pursued by Porsche designers can be said to have been the Gran Turismo (Grand Touring) type; a high-performance vehicle capable of long-distance, high-speed touring in safety and comfort (in contrast to the Sport Car, or the sports car in the narrow sense of the term). Hence, from the outset, they gave more than due consideration to ensuring riding comfort, an aspect so far neglected in sports cars. It was for this reason that

23

The tough structure of the Porsche 356, with a platform chassis built of steel plates, which was light in weight and high in rigidity
This picture shows the earliest model. The front axle, brakes, steering, gearbox, etc. were those of the stock Volkswagen.

the aerodynamic two-plus-two coupé was selected as the basic body design for the Porsche, instead of the open two-seater type which was considered the orthodox sports car style of that period. As already mentioned, Dr. Porsche did not take part in the actual designing of the 356, but since the Volkswagen was the basis for the 356, his design concepts were incorporated into the car. Important features of the 356 were: (1) Platform chassis, which was light in weight and high in rigidity; (2) Independent front and rear suspensions based on torsion bars (double trailing arm for the front wheels, and radius arms and swing axles for the rear wheels); (3) Lightweight and compact, air-cooled, horizontally opposed, 4-cylinder rear engine; (4) Aerodynamic body, covering the engine and other mechanical parts as compactly as possible, yet providing sufficient room for two seats and an ample trunk for storing baggage necessary for long-distance touring.

Let us suppose a person accustomed to driving an MG or Triumph chanced to get into a Porsche 356 for the first time. What would surprise him first would be the roomy cockpit, which was as comfortable as that of an elegant sedan. Next, he would be impressed with the solid build of the body, as evidenced by the pleasant metallic "click" made by the thick door as it closed as if under its own weight. As soon as the car started rolling, he would notice that all controls, such as steering, gear shift, and clutch, were incomparably light. As the engine, which was placed at the rear, was accelerated, it would softly whir, accompanied with the characteristic sound of the fan; and the driver would become aware of the total absence of vibration usually found in an in-line 4-cylinder engine. At high speeds he would notice that there was almost no wind noise, which was always audible in an open MG or TR-2, and he could be made uneasy by the unusual stillness. Compared to the MG and the TR-2 whose strength was in the lower engine speed ranges, the 356 was more comfortable in the higher engine speeds. In fact when the car was in top gear it was actually in an overdrive, so that frequent gear shifting was required. In compensation for this inconvenience, however, the 356 could run in top gear for long periods of time. On the Autobahn, for instance, the Porche 356, as compared with small sports cars of England, could maintain a surprisingly high average speed.

And what smooth riding this car would give! Even on bad roads it could maintain speeds unlikely with cars like the MG. (A passenger in an MG might feel nervous lest a door should open at any moment, but the Porsche's body would not even creak.) Its steering was light and very responsive. A driver accustomed to an MG or a Triumph could lose his feel for driving when he was in a Porsche, which would run smoothly and quietly. He might approach corners at excessive speeds and, glancing at the speedometer, become so shocked, be might hurriedly release the accelerator. Then the combined effects of the swing axle and the narrow tires (the tire width of the early Porsche was the same as that of the Volkswagen: 5.00—16), would cause the tail to slide. If the driver was not used to the car, he could go into a complete spin, and become thoroughly disgusted with it.

An early model of the 356 certainly had a strong tendency to oversteer, and it was said to be unable to take high-speed corners by drifting. It is a fact that, even at lesser road speeds, the car required considerable driving skill. Its weight distribution was about 42/58, even with two riders, and the rear wheels had a negative camber of over two degrees. The tires were unbelievably undersized by today's standards, so that in the final analysis the above mentioned behavior should not be unexpected. According to Porsche designers, final oversteer was safer than excessive understeer (which was the case with most other cars of those days).

However, as production of the Porsche 356 increased, and as increasing numbers of cars of this type were purchased by drivers of ordinary skill, problems of handling began to crop up. From the standpoint of maneuverability, the process of development of the Porsche 356 can be summarized as an effort to tame the car — i.e. to make the sharp oversteer of early Porsches, approach neutral steering and, finally, to make it return, gradually, to oversteer. The 356 front suspension was identical to that of the Volkswagen, and there were no stabilizers in the models preceding that of 1954. This latter model, being equipped with stabilizers, had higher roll stiffness at the front and a lesser tendency to oversteer.

Concerning this aspect, an epoch-making improvement was made in one of the later 356 series, the 356 B Super-90 of 1959. A lateral leaf spring was added at the rear, and at the same time weaker torsion bars (reduced from .95 in. to .91 in. in diameter) were attached. The leaf spring was supported at the center so that it might roll freely on the central pivot. When the body rolled during cornering, the leaf spring would simply incline with the center as the axis, and it would perform hardly any spring action. It would bend only when it was under full load or when both wheels bounced simultaneously over rough surfaces. Thanks to this compensator spring, which would not work during cornering, weaker torsion bars could be substituted; and, accordingly, part of the cornering load, which had formerly been sustained at the rear, could be shifted to the front. As a result, the side force heretofore received by the rear tire decreased, and the tendency to oversteer was diminished (in exchange for somewhat greater rolling). As a matter of fact, the 356 B Super-90 is said to have been the first Porsche car that enabled the driver to use the so-called drifting technique for cornering (which, in other words, is to change understeer to oversteer by using power).

What divided the public evaluation of the Porsche was, quite ironically, also

Cross section of the 356A, showing the roomy space for two passengers and the compact air-cooled, horizontally opposed engine placed behind the rear axle
This basic layout did not change during the 17-year-long process of development of the 356 series.

the fact that the car was such a precision machine. The machining precision of its air-cooled engine, for example, was more like that of a racing engine than of a utility car engine. No gasket was used between the cylinder block and the cylinder head, and so long as proper tightening torque and order were followed, no gas leakage was possible between the metal surfaces. The clearance between the piston and the cylinder, when both were of light alloy as in the case of the Super model, was only about 0.015–0.025 mm. Compared with this, the clearance in the case of the MG Midget, for example, was as much as 0.040–0.056 mm. Special knowledge and special tools were necessary for repair work, and about all an ordinary car owner could do was stick his head into the small hatch to adjust the fan belt or replace the plugs (which was rather a troublesome job, and he was obliged to use a particular wrench provided with the car). Even to adjust a tappet, he could work only from underneath the car. Accordingly, lovers of English sports cars, who would park their cars at the roadside and nonchalantaly engage in a large-scale overhaul with nothing but simple hand tools and common sense, would find the Porsche quite beyond their power — and often beyond their means. It was quite likely, then, that many of them, out of spite, spoke against Porsche cars.

If the MG and the Triumph were the sports cars for the physically strong, the Porsche was the sports car for the intellectual. To be able to tame the Porsche, one required not physical strength but a sharp reflex, delicate nerves, and a love for the car backed up by a proper knowledge of its engineering. It was people engaged in intellectual occupations that were attracted by the Porsche. This fact clearly shows the intrinsic characteristics of the Porsche.

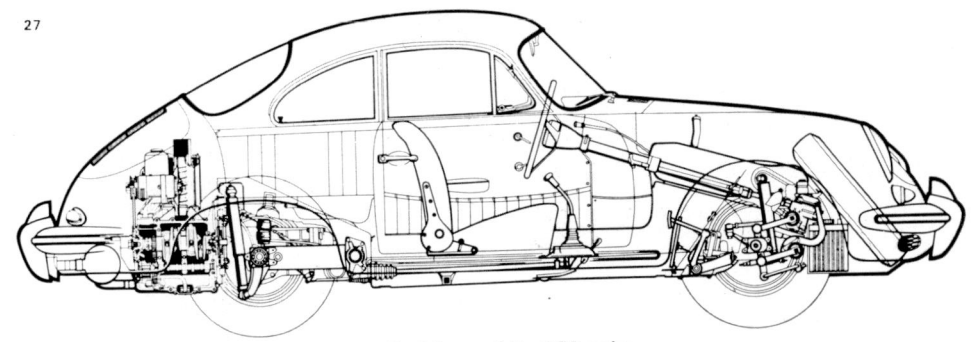

Cross section of the 356 C, showing the final form of the 356 series
There was no change in the basic form, except for small details. But the performance, especially the maneuverability, was improved tremendously. The wheelbase remained the same at 82.7 in., but the weight was increased from the initial 1,642 lbs. (356 coupé) to the final 2,061 lbs. (356 C coupé).

Cross section of the 1500 S engine, 1952—1955
This engine was a high-performance type with a built-up crankshaft, made by Hirth, and needle-roller big ends.

Porsche 356 Prototype No. 2, built in the fall of 1948
This car already had the characteristic style of the 356 series coupé, the production of which lasted for nearly twenty years.

Porsche 356 Prototype No. 1
This car is now preserved in the Porsche Museum.

Porsche 356 Prototype No. 2
The man standing behind it is Dr. Anton Piëch, Dr. Porsche's partner.

Changes in the 356 Series

The prototype No. 1 of the 356 was built in the summer of 1948. It had a style not much different from models produced later — a two-seater roadster with a specially designed platform chassis of very stiff box-section. The suspension, brakes, and steering system were however, the same as those of the stock Volkswagen. The engine and the unsynchronized transmission also were the same as those of an early model of the Volkswagen. The engine capacity was 1,131 cc, and the compression ratio was raised to 7.0:1. With two Solex carburetors, the engine developed an output of 40 HP. Of special note was that the engine was placed in front of the rear axle.

Next came the prototype No. 2, which was a coupé. Its overall shape and the location of its engine (overhung behind the rear axle to provide trunk room) were like those of the production models that followed. Thorough running tests were repeated with this prototype by Ferry Porsche and other designers (mostly on alpine roads, including the Grossglockner Pass, which were near the workshop).

At about the same time, on September 17, 1948, a very important contract was concluded between the Porsche and Volkswagen companies. According to this contract, which in broad outline is still effective today, "Porsche was not allowed to design a car for another company if it was likely to become competitive with the current Volkswagen type. Volkswagen was entitled to freely use any of the Porsche patents, but had to pay Porsche a royalty for each Volkswagen manufactured. Porsche, on the other hand, could freely use Volkswagen parts to build sports cars and could also make use of the Volkswagen service chain." It was indeed fortunate for Porsche to have signed this contract, for it enabled the newborn company to secure a stable source of income and, what was more, to utilize the Volkswagen service network which extended all over the world.

Type 356, 1948–1955

Series production of the 356 was started on a small scale in the winter of 1948–49. A total of fity cars were built. Except for six with cabriolet bodywork by the Beutler Company of Switzerland, they all had aluminum coupé bodies that were entirely hand-processed. It was this semi-production model, built at Gmünd, that was exhibited for the first time at the Geneva Show of 1948. The triangular vents on the doors served to distinguish this model from the later models manufactured in Stuttgart.

Full-scale production of the 356 began in the spring of 1950, in a rented space of 598 square yards in one of the workshops of the Reutter Company in Zuffenhausen, on the outskirts of Stuttgart. Only one model, the 356/1100 (369), was manufactured and offered in coupé and cabriolet styles. According to the first leaflet introducing this model, its engine capacity, like that of the Volkswagen, was 1,131 cc. Actually, however, in order to qualify for the 1,100-cc racing class, it was reduced to 1,086 cc (73.5 x 64 mm), with a compression ratio of 7:1, an output of 40 (D.I.N.) HP/4,200 rpm, and a torque of 51.7 lb. ft/2,800 rpm. Many of the parts, such as the partitioned crankcase, crashbox, and front axle, were common with those of the Volkswagen. The brakes were also the same as those of the stock Volkswagen, and both the front and rear brakes were leading-trailing shoes with 9.06 inches diameter drums. The wheels had 4 J x 16 rims and 5.00–16 tires.

The body was not much different in shape from that of the model built at Gmünd, but being of steel it slightly increased the car's weight to 1,642 pounds. The leaflet also mentioned the maximum speed to be 87 mph., and the fuel consumption was over 30 miles per gallon. In the first production year, 410 cars were manufactured, and more than half of them quickly found buyers in various countries.

In 1951, besides the 1100 model, the 1300 (506) and the 1500 (527) were added to the production line. The engine of the 1300 model had a capacity of 1,286 cc (80 x 64 mm), a compression ratio of 6.5:1, an output of 44 HP/4,200 rpm, and a torque of 59.7 lb.ft./2,800 rpm. The 1500 model had a 1,488-cc (80 x 74 mm) engine with a compression ratio of 7:1. Its connecting rod big end had a roller bearing, and the crankshaft was a built-up type made by the Hirth Company, well known for its aircraft engines. The output was 60 HP/5,000 rpm, and the torque was 75.2 lb.ft./3,000 rpm. These two new models had maximum speeds of 90 mph and 96 mph, respectively. Unlike the Volkswagen and the 356/1100, which had cast iron cylinders, the new models had light-alloy cylinders with chrome-plated inner surfaces. Beginning that year, the front brakes were changed to two-leading shoes, and their wheels received vents. Production of the 1300 was continued until January, 1954, and that of the 1500 until September, 1952.

In the Le Mans race of 1951, an 1100 coupé made a formal entry as a Works car for the first time. With a French driver it won the 1,100-cc class race and placed twentieth in the overall classification, and thus Porsche made a successful debut in racing, marking also the first postwar comeback of German cars. For the Liège-Rome-Liège Rally held in August of the same year, Porsche entered two cars, an 1100 and a 1500. The former, driven by von Hanstein, was second, while the latter won the 1,500-cc class. In that year Porsche produced a total of 1,103 cars.

In September, 1952, two new models of the 1500 were announced: the 1500 S (528) and the 1500 (546). The former was a high-performance version fitted

First leaflet, published in the summer of 1948
The pictures, probably drawn with the prototype No. 2 coupé as the model, were not quite true to the actual production model. The leaflet stated that the car weighed 1,323 lbs. and was good for 87 mph.

33 Porsche 356 with a hand-processed aluminum coupé body
Fifty units of this model were built at Gmünd. The center pillar on the windshield, the triangular vents on the doors, the wheels without vents, etc. served to distinguish this car from later models of the 356.

34 Porsche 356 coupés built at Gmünd
This photograph shows units of the coupé, with the front and rear wheels covered, being driven from Stuttgart Plant to France for participation at Le Mans. The engines were tuned for 44 HP.

35 Owing to an accident during practice, only one of the above cars participated in the race at Le Mans, 1951.

with a 1,488-cc engine, a built-up crankshaft and roller bearings, and developed 70 HP/5,000 rpm with a compression ratio of 8.2:1. The latter model, also called the "Damen," was intended for gentlewomen drivers. It had plain bearings and developed 55 HP/4,400 rpm. Their maximum speeds were 103 mph and 93 mph, respectively. As for the gearbox, the famous Porsche-patented self-servo-synchromatic transmission became standard on both of these models, and gear shifting became virtually foolproof. These two 1500 models were produced until November, 1954.

In November, 1953, the 1300 S (589), a high-performance version of the 1300, made its appearance. Its engine was completely different from that of the previous model, 1300 (506). Its capacity was 1,290 cc (74.5 x 74 mm), compression ratio 8.2:1, output 60 HP/5,500 rpm, and torque 65 lb.ft./3,600 rpm. Its sport cam with 38-degree overlap (while the normal cam had an unusually low five degrees) was common with the 1500 S. The car developed a maximum speed of 99 mph, which was outstandingly quick for the 1,300 class.

Until 1954, the type 356 came only in coupé and cabriolet styles. But in this year the two-seater Speedster appeared and immediately gained popularity among America's west coast racing drivers. As a matter of fact, this car was preceded in 1952 by the open two-seater model named the "America Roadster," which had very low doors and a removable windshield. Only twenty units of this model were built at that time. Except for the body, the Speedster was the same as the other models of the 356, but it weighed less by as much as 154 pounds. Around this period, the 356 was available in five models: the 1100, 1300, 1300 S, 1500, and 1500 S, but the Speedster could be ordered only in the 1500 and 1500 S models. The gearbox of the Speedster had lower third and fourth gear speeds than those of the coupé or the cabriolet, which meant better acceleration but a somewhat lower top speed. The performance of the Speedster with a 70 HP engine was 17.4 seconds in the standing start 400 meters, with a top speed of 106 mph, while that of the coupé with the same engine was 18.4 seconds and 109 mph.

Improvements made in connection with

Porsche 356 "America Roadster," 1952
This photograph shows a forerunner model of the Speedster, which was to appear in 1954.

Porsche 356 Coupé, 1952—1955
This was a late model of the 356 series with a completely machine-pressed body.

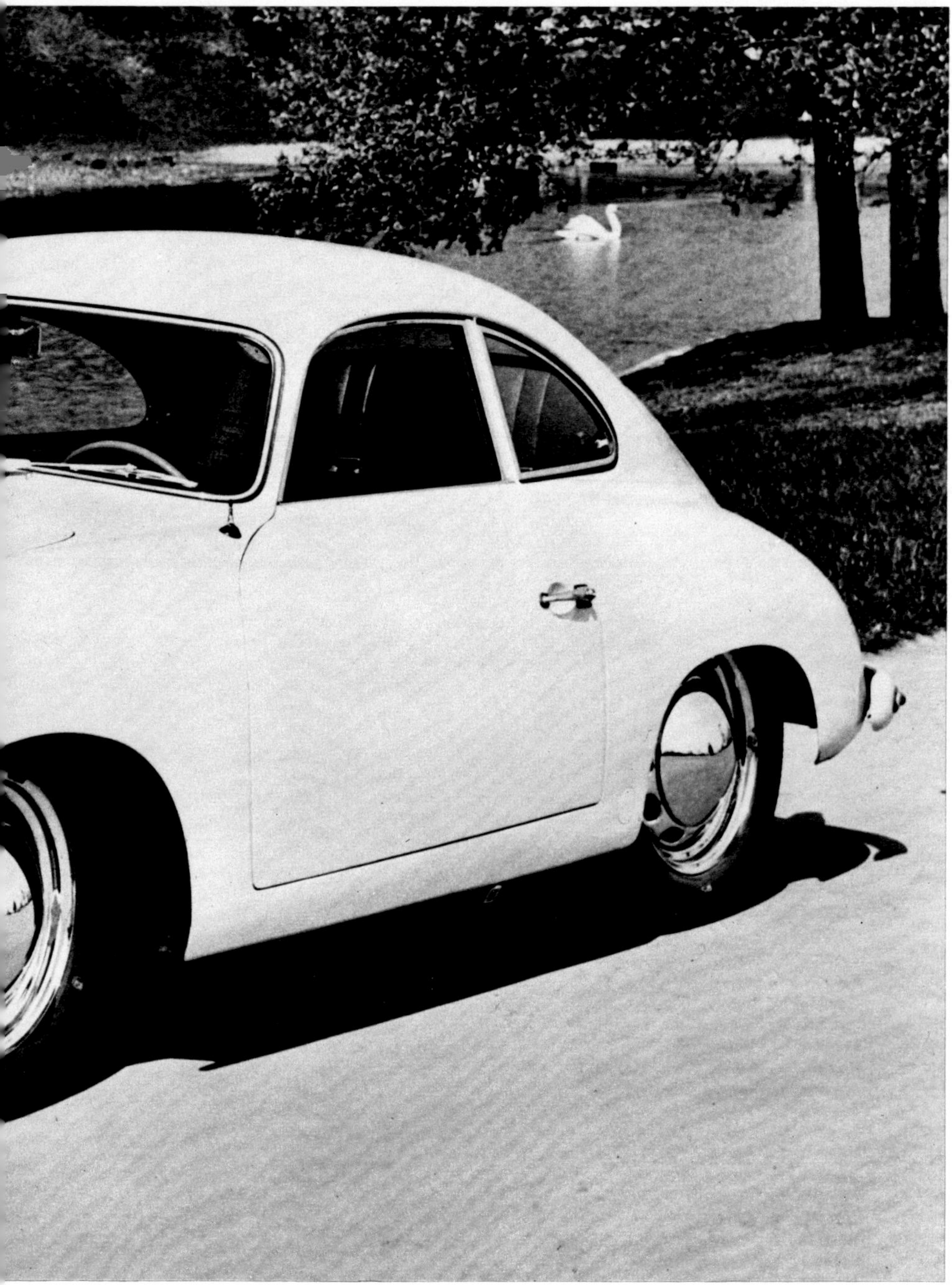

Porsche 356 Cabriolet, 1952—1955
The cabriolet with a thick, lined folding top was characteristic of German cars. Its weather protection was almost as good as that of the coupé.

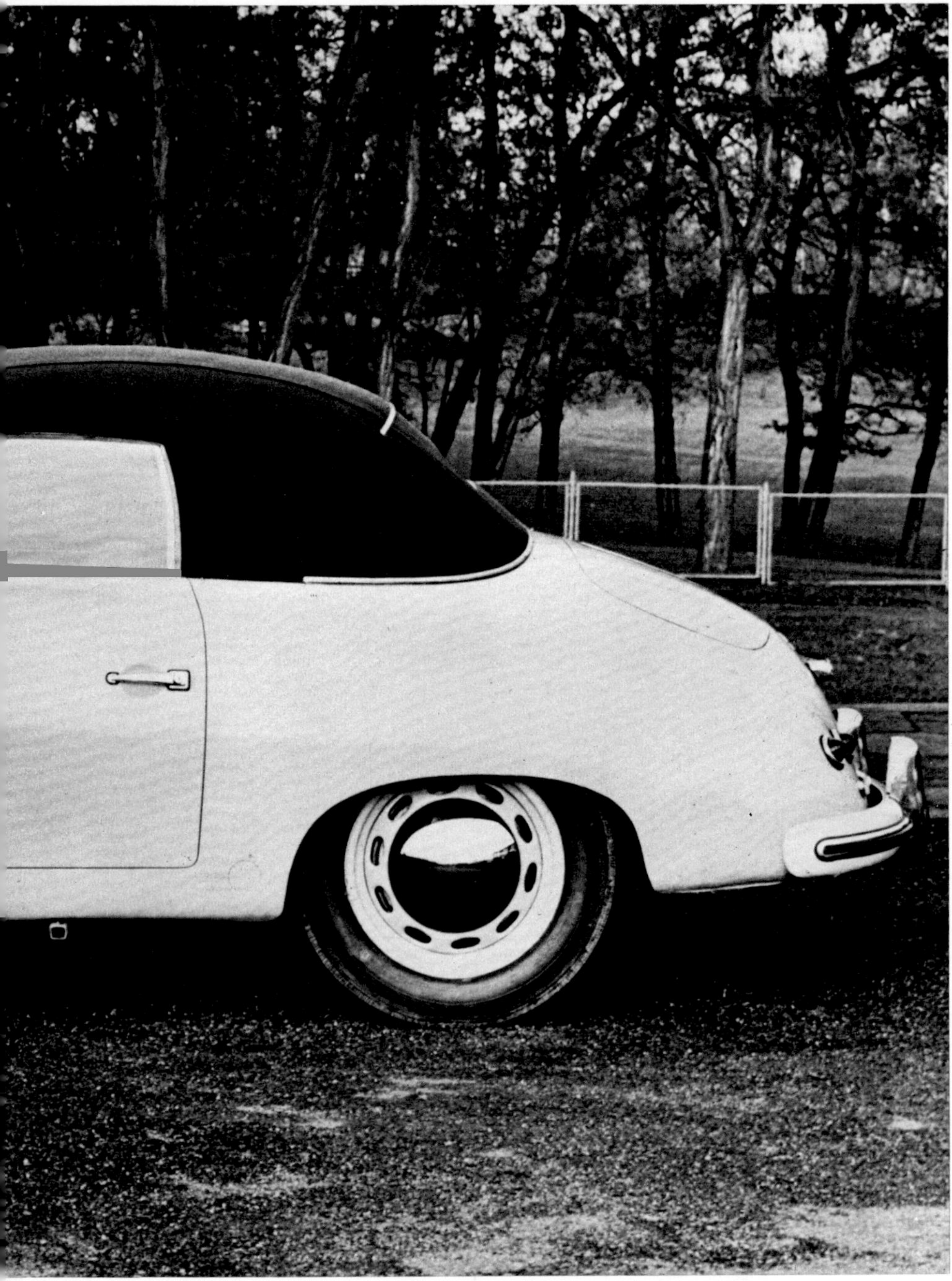

Porsche 356 Cabriolet, 1952—1955
The thick top could be folded in neatly, offering practically no obstruction of the rear view.

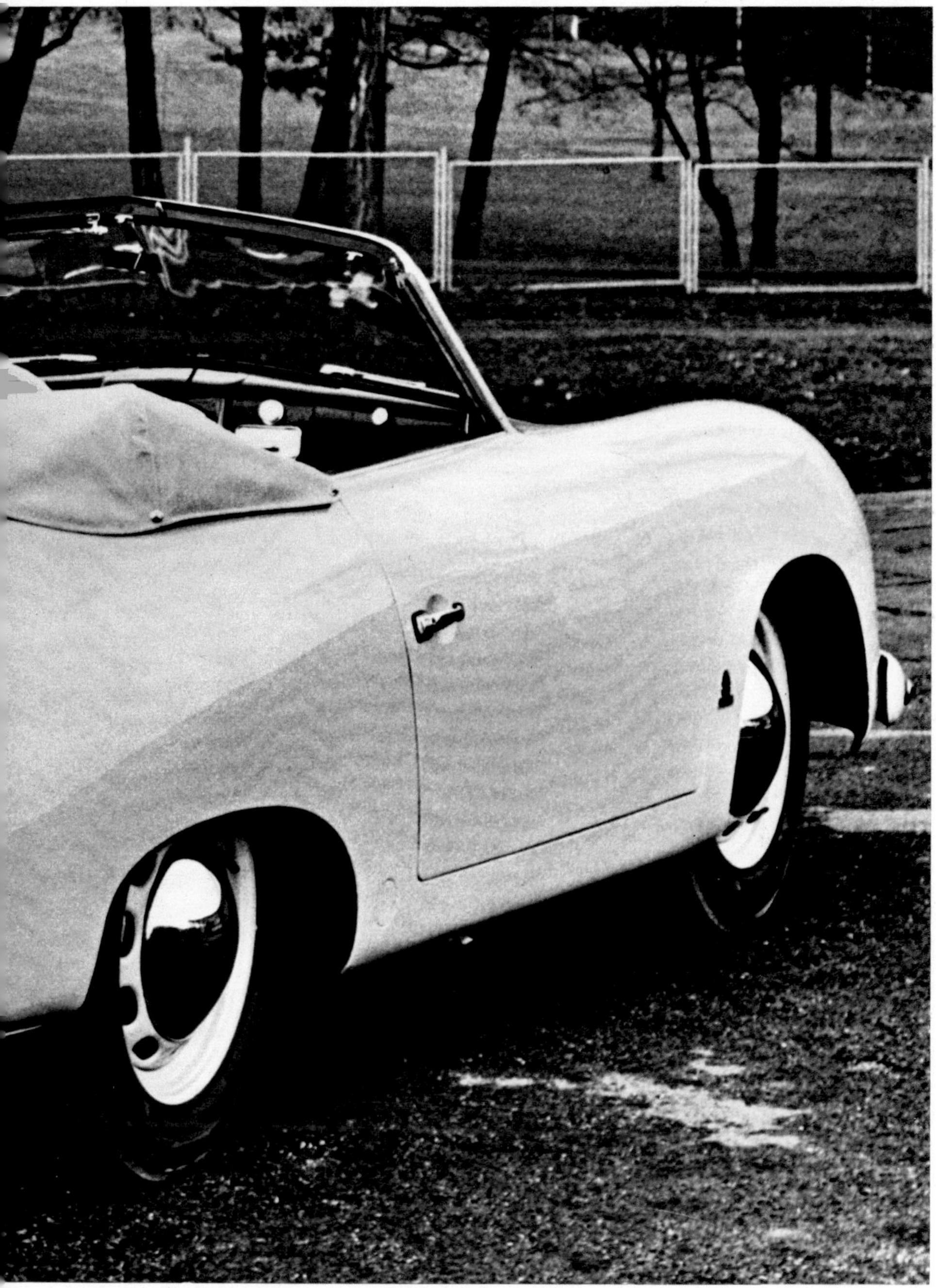

Interesting photograph of the Porsche factory in 1953
The view shows processing of crankcases and gear cases. To the left can be seen two-piece crankcases, which were still common with those of the Volkswagen.

41

Assembly line, about 1953
Bodies which arrived completely painted from the coach builder were placed on trolleys, and parts were carefully assembled on to them as the bodies were pushed along by men.

Engine assembly section, about 1953
There were no assembly lines here. Each skilled worker assembled an engine from beginning to end, assuming complete responsibility.

the chassis of the Speedster were: the front axles were strengthened, torsion-bar stabilizers were attached, and, accordingly, oversteer decreased slightly. In November, 1954, the 1300 (506/2), a de-tuned version of the 1300 S, appeared to replace the older model 1300 (506). This was a rather tame model, fitted with an engine having a capacity of 1,290 cc, a compression ratio of 6.5:1, and an output of 44 HP/4,200 rpm. Beginning with this new variation of the 1300, all Porsche cars were fitted with a crankcase different from that of the Volkswagen, which was a three-section type with a separate timing case at the front end.

Type 356 A, 1956–1959

In October, 1955, the 356 A, a new variation of the 356, appeared as the '56 model. There was a very slight change in its external appearance — the V-shaped windshield was replaced by a wider, curved one — but there were considerable changes internally. In connection with the chassis; the torsion-bar mounting became adjustable, both the stabilizers and the dampers were strengthened, the nylon bushes in the suspension arms were changed to needle roller bearings, the handbrake became a lever type, the wheel size became 4.5 J x 15 and the tire size became 5.60—15. In the interior: a horn ring was attached to the steering wheel, the blinker became an automatic cut-off type, the windshield jet became foot-operated and the dashboard was covered with a crash pad for the first time.

The 1500 series came to an end in this year, and in its place appeared the 1600 and the 1600 S. The 1600 (616/1) was fitted with a 1,582-cc (82.5 x 74 mm) engine having a compression ratio of 7.5:1, and an output of 60 HP/4,500 rpm, while the 1600 S (616/2) had a compression ratio of 8.5:1 and an output of 75 HP/5,000 rpm. In contrast to the 1500 S, which had roller bearings and a built-up crankshaft, the 1600 S had ordinary plain bearings. Its bodywork came in three styles: coupé, cabriolet, and speedster. The maximum speed of the 60-HP 1600 model was 99 mph, and that of the 75-HP 1600 S was 109 mph.

The '57 model, which made its debut at the 1957 Frankfurt Show, had the following improvements: the steering was changed from the screw type to the ZF worm type (which was built up after a running-in equivalent of about 3,000 miles); the floor was strengthened to allow the attachement of seat belts, etc. Beginning in 1957, the 1600 (616/1 T-2) engine had cast iron cylinders. The carburetor was changed from Solex to Zenith 32 NDIX double choke, and as a result its flexibility increased. Clutching became smoother and the gear-shift mechanism was improved at the same time, so that shift lever movement became shorter. Production of the 1300, which lasted for many years, was stopped in September 1957.

The 1958 model, except for the strengthened front axles, was structurally unchanged but appeared in two new body styles. First of all, the Speedster was dropped, and the Convertible D (the "D" stood for Drauz, the body builder) appeared. It was a two-seater having the same body as that of the Speedster, but it was fitted with a lined calash top and

43

Porsche 356 A Coupé, 1956–1959

roll-up windows. The other style was the cabriolet with a removable hardtop made by Karmann. Back in 1950, when the manufacture of the 356 went to full scale, a total of only 410 cars were turned out, but in 1958, 5,160 units of the 1600 and the 1600 S left the Stuttgart plant for markets all over the world. The breakdown of this total was 3,700 coupés, 380 cabriolets and hardtops, and 1,100 Speedsters and Convertible D's.

Type 356 B, 1959—1962

The 356 B, which made its debut at the 1959 Frankfurt Show, was marked by considerable change to its front area. Reflecting the worsening traffic conditions in urban districts, the front and rear bumpers were raised by nearly four inches, and bumper guards became standard attachments. The headlight position became higher and, accordingly, the fenders also become higher. Moreover, air intakes for cooling the front-wheel brakes were provided under the bumper. In the interior: the steering wheel took a "dished" form in black plastic, a convenient switch serving as both the light and blinker switch was attached, and a defroster was provided for the rear window. In connection with the chassis, a marked improvement was made in the brakes, which were provided with cast iron liners integrally cast into fin-cooled light-alloy drums.

The engine for the 1600 series was, up to this time, available in two types: 60 HP and 75 HP. Beginning with the 356 B, a more powerful engine, called Super 90, was added. This engine had an output of 90 HP/5,500 rpm and a torque of 89 lb.ft./4,300 rpm. The 1600 S-90 replaced the very expensive 356 A/1500 G Carrera with a DOHC 110 HP engine, the production of which had been discontinued the previous year. Its price of $3,780 was $2,000 lower than that of the Carrera, but its performance was said to be about the same. Top speed was 115 mph and the 0-400 meters time

Porsche 356 A Speedster, 1956—1957

Porsche 356 A Convertible D

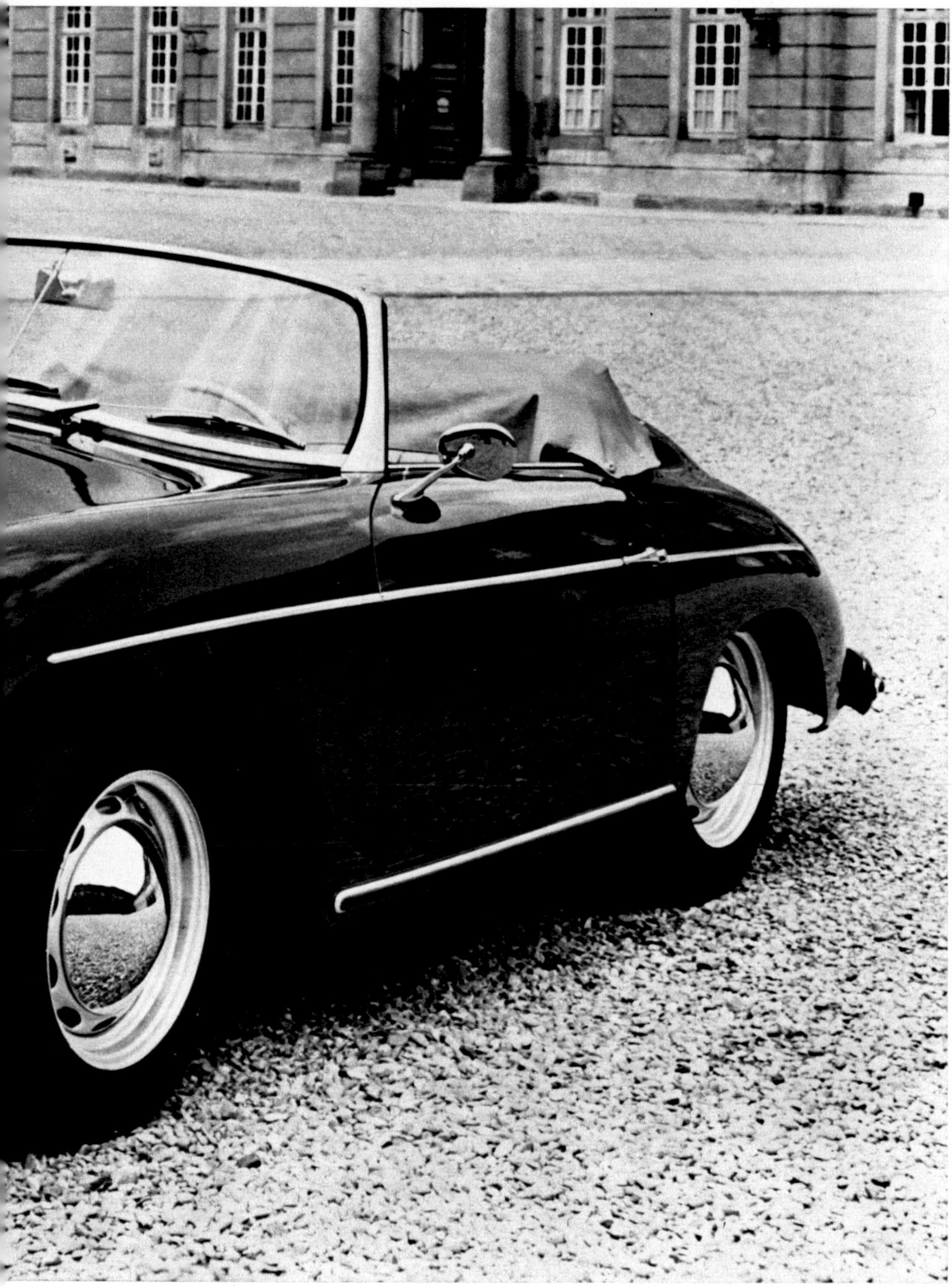

Porsche 356 A convertible D

Porsche 356 A Cabriolet
This rear view of the Cabriolet is shown for comparison with the photograph above. The triangular vents, a roundish folding top, and absence of chrome stripes on the body sides differentiate this car from the Convertible D.

was 17.5 seconds.

The S-90 engine, which differed greatly from the engines for the other 1600 series, had special light-alloy cylinders with molybdenum steel, called "Ferral", electrochemically deposited on the bore surfaces. The rocker arms and the push rods also were made of light alloy so as to reduce their inertial mass. Regarding the chassis, as mentioned before, a supplementary leaf spring was added to the rear axle, and the torsion bars were weakened so as to shift some of the cornering load from the rear wheels to the front wheels, thereby retaining the understeer throughout the speed range. 165-15 radial tires became standard for the S-90. There were absolutely no changes in the '60 and '61 models. With the '62 model slight changes were made; mainly in the body. First, with the coupé, the front and rear window areas were enlarged, the ventilation system was improved, and an air intake was provided directly in front of the windshield. Moreover, a fuel filler was provided in the front fender at the right side, so that it became possible to refuel without opening the hood. In addition, two air inlets, instead of one, were made in the engine cover. As for body style, the Convertible D was renamed the Roadster and was produced till 1962. In the same year a new model with a fixed hardtop (made by Karmann) appeared, but its production was discontinued within the year.

Type 356 C, 1963–1965

The 356 C, the final model in the development of the 356 series, appeared in 1963 and was manufactured until May, 1965. The 356 B 1600 Normal was replaced by two higher-class models, the 1600 C and the 1600 SC. The

Porsche 356 B Coupé
The emblem in the center of each wheel cap was a feature only of the 356 B.

Porsche 356 B Cabriolet, 1962

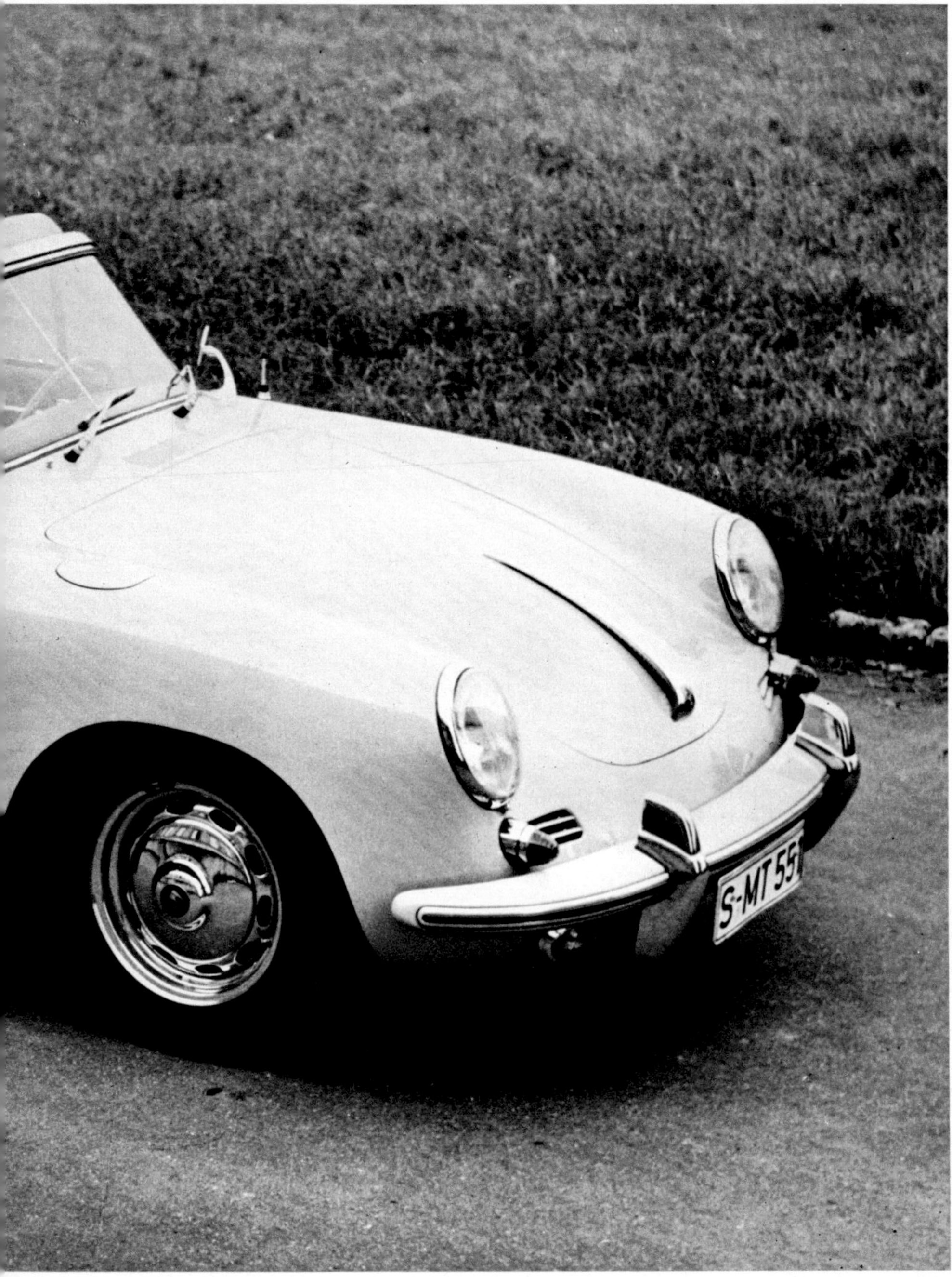
S-MT 55

Cabriolet with a removable hardtop

From left to right: the combined guage for oil temperature and fuel; the revolution counter, which would register up to 6,000; and the speedometer, which would read up to 200 km/h. The car had unusually wide leg room for a sports car

The Autobahn Police of West Germany have long been a customer of Porsche. The car shown was a regular production model listed in the catalogue.

Tail of the 356 B, remodeled in 1962. The car in the foreground is the new model, showing the remodeled tail with two ventilating grilles and an enlarged rear window.

former had a 75 HP/5,200 rpm engine, with a compression ratio of 8.5:1, while the latter had a 95 HP/5,800 rpm engine with a compression ratio of 9.5:1. Both were high-performance vehicles comparable to the previous S-90. With the 356 C, the greatest improvement was seen in its brakes, for Porsche finally decided to adopt four-wheel disc brakes. This was an opposed piston type designed by ATE of Germany under license from Dunlop, and the rear wheel discs had small-diameter drums built in for the hand-brake. The effective disc diameters were 8.9 inches for the front and 9.57 inches for the rear. The supplementary leaf spring for the rear axle, which was standard for the 356 B S-90, became optional for both the 1600 C and the 1600 SC models. Maximum speeds were 109 mph for the 1600 C and 115 mph for the 1600 SC, and the time for SS 1 km was 34.8 and 33.2 seconds, respectively. These figures meant outstandingly high performance for the 1,600-cc class of GT cars with complete touring equipment.

The 356 Porsche, which was born in 1948 based on the Volkswagen (which was designed and built for the masses), went through seventeen years of constant improvement, and finally matured into a thoroughbred sports car of the highest caliber in all aspects. To make further developments, it was necessary for the Porsche designers to abandon the basic Volkswagen based layout and to approach the design from an entirely new angle.

Disc brake on a rear wheel of the 356
The 356 C was the first Porsche car with four-wheel disc brakes.

356 C/1600 C/1600 SC, 1963 – 1965
This is a model at the final stage of development of

54

he 356 series.

CHAPTER 3
The Early Carrera and Renn Sport (1953—1963)

From the 356 A/1500 GS Carrera to the 356 B/2000 GS

Even the 356 Normal, the tamest of the Type 356 series, was an authentic sports car. But the Porsche Company itself considered its early models (including the 356 C/1600 S) as merely fast touring cars. Porsche's idea of a sports car was the Carrera and the RS Spyder, which will be described next.

Almost from the time of its establishment, Porsche enthusiastically took part in international races and rallies. Of the cars used for this purpose, particularly active were the GT Carreras for the GT class, and a series of RS (Renn Sport) Spyders for the Sports Car class. Since these cars were all based on the 1,500—1,600-cc production models of the 356, they were always at a disadvantage at racing tracks such as Le Mans, Monza and the Nürburgring, where they fought valiantly against cars like Ferrari, Aston Martin, Jaguar, and Maserati, all of which had nearly twice the engine displacement. But at a few circuits, including the Targa Florio, where cornering and braking efficiency counted more than absolute speed, the Porsche cars displayed overwhelming strength, particularly from 1956 onwards. During those few seasons immediately preceding 1962, they won overall Targa victories in 1956, 1959, and 1960. Also, in the Sports-Car Manufacturer's Championship series of races, the same models placed second behind a Ferrari in 1960 and 1962. In other words, the Carrera and the RS, fitted with mere 1.6 — 2 liter 4-cylinder engines, actually beat the 3-liter V-12 Ferrari Testa Rosa.

Until the early sixties, when racing was not so specialized or so highly commercialized as it is today, these Porsche Works cars (the Carrera and the RS), almost without any modifications, were built as a production model series and were available to all customers. (Even today the 917, for example, is in principle a "production model" with limited production of 25 units, but this term was used in a different sense in those days.)

In 1954 a Porsche coupé took part in the Liège-Rome-Liège Rally and attracted much attention by winning the 1,500-cc class. At a glance one would have thought it just an ordinary production model, but it was fitted with a 4-camshaft racing engine from the Renn Sport 550 Spyder. This car was the prototype of the Carrera, which, in the ten years that followed, made the name of Porsche renowened in GT races and rallies.

The Carrera, which in the fall of 1955 formally became a production model with the name of 356 A/1500 G, was indeed a wolf in sheep's clothing. Its engine was entirely different from that of the usual 356 A/1600; it was a racing type 550 Spyder engine, de-tuned for easier handling. Its light-alloy cylinders had a

356 A/1500 GS Carrera "Deluxe"

Four-camshft engine of the 1600 GS Carrera, 1959—1960
This was a DOHC 1,588-cc engine, tuned for either 105 HP/6,500 rpm or 115 HP/6,500 rpm.

356 B/1600 GTL Carrera-Abarth, 1960
This model was active in racing until about 1964.

capacity of 1,498 cc (85 x 66 mm) and a compression ratio of 9:1. It was provided with valves arranged in "V" angle and operated by four shaft-driven overhead camshafts, a double ignition system, and a dry sump. All bearings were roller type, which meant that the crankshaft was a built-up type made by the Hirth Company. The engine output was of two levels: 100 HP/6,200 rpm for the Carrera Deluxe and 110 HP/6,400 rpm for the Gran Turismo. The latter car was solely for racing, and efforts were made to reduce the car's weight as much as possible. It was fitted with light-alloy doors and hood, acrylic resin window panes, and simplified interiors, so that it weighed 143 pounds less than the Deluxe version. The brakes, too, were different. Large drums with the same diameter as that of the 550 Spyder were used in the front. The 110-HP Gran Turismo covered the SS ¼mile in 16.5 seconds and developed a maximum speed of 124 mph — outstandingly high performance for a 1,500-cc class production model. Even the 100-HP Deluxe coupé attained a maximum speed of nearly 124 mph with 17.5 seconds for the SS ¼ mile, and yet one could enjoy the same riding comfort as in the 356 A Normal.

In 1959 the 1600 GS and the 1600 GT appeared with an enlarged 1,588-cc (87.5 x 66 mm) engine, which had plain bearings instead of roller bearings. The output of these cars was 105 HP/6,500 rpm and 115 HP/6,500 rpm, respectively. So far as their performance was concerned, they differed little from the 1500 GS/GT of the previous year, but the adoption of plain bearings greatly reduced the engine noise.

With the appearance of the 356 B in the same year, production of the Carrera was stopped temporarily, but a limited run of 60 units was produced in 1960. Of these, 40 units were fitted with ordinary bodies made by Reutter, while the remaining 20 units were sent in chassis form to Abarth in Turin, where light-alloy bodies of characteristic styling were fitted. These were called the 356 B/1600 GTL Carrera-Abarth. To obtain sufficient rigidity, the body of this model was made of light alloy but

Carrera-Abarth 2000 GS-GT
This is a snapshot of the car winning the GT race at Solitude in 1963. The driver was Joachim Bonnier.

Carrera 2000 GS, or Carrera 2, 1962–1965
This is the car von Hanstein drove at the First Grand Prix of Japan at Suzuka in May, 1962. With completely standard equipment, it averaged 79 mph.

weighed about the same as one made of steel. Because of its small frontal area, however, the car developed a top speed of 137 mph. Although the Carrera 1600 was priced rather high at $6,000, about 700 units were manufactured before production was temporarily stopped the following year.

The name "Carrera" reappeared in the fall of 1961 on a new model which was called the Carrera 2000 GS (or, simply, the Carrera 2). This vehicle had a body-shell from the 356 B/1600

60

DOHC 1,966-cc engine of the Carrera 2000 GS

Carrera 2000 GS with author, photographed at Solitude Circuit in the summer of 1964

S-90 and a 4-camshaft sport racing engine from the RS 61, which had a capacity of 1,966 cc (92 x 74 mm) and an output of 130 HP/6,200 rpm. Having a maximum speed of 124 mph and requiring only 8.9 seconds to reach a speed of over 60 mph, it was the most powerful, high-performance Porsche road car. Its front brakes were of the disc type which had developed from that of the F-2 Porsche (to be described later), and the calipers were attached, not to the hubs, but to the wheel carriers. It was this Carrera 2 that participated in the First Japanese Grand Prix held at the Suzuka Circuit in May, 1962. Driven by von Hastein, Porsche's racing manager, it registered a best lap time of two minutes 47 seconds and an average speed of 79 mph for the race. As for the Carrera-Abarth mentioned earlier, it was later fitted with a 2-liter Carrera-2 engine and was renamed the Carrera 2000 GS-GT. This car continued to show good results in the GT prototype class until about 1964.

RS (Renn Sport)

Let us now go back a little to 1950. A man named Gloeckler, who was a sportsman and a Volkswagen/Porsche dealer in Frankfurt, remodeled a 356/1100 car and fitted it with an OHC engine tuned to produce 90 HP. With this rebuilt car he took part in domestic races and obtained brilliant results. The designers at Porsche were deeply impressed by this special car and decided to build a Porsche sports/racing car. Thus, the Type 550 Spyder came into being.

It being evident that the existing push-rod OHV production engines were unsuitable for racing purposes, they specially designed for the new model a shaft-driven 4-camshaft engine, which was named Type 547. It had a capacity of 1,498-cc (85 x 66 mm), a compression ratio of 9:1, and an output of 110 HP/6,200 rpm. It was provided with twin Solex 40 P 11-4 carburetors and all bearings were of needle-roller type.

In the spring of 1953, when Porsche decided to enter the 550 Spyder in the Nürburgring race of the same year, its Type 547 engine was not yet sufficiently developed for racing. Accordingly, Porsche mounted a tuned 1,500S OHV engine on the chassis of the prototype 550 Spyder. Driven by Gloeckler, this vehicle brilliantly won the race by defeating Borgward's works car. Two 550 Spyders, both of which had a coupé top on the same chassis, participated in the Le Mans race the same year. The car driven by Paul Frere/Frankenberg attained a speed of 123 mph on the Mulsanne straight and won the 1,500-cc class with an average speed of 86 mph.

The 550 Spyder, fitted with a 4-camshaft racing engine, made a splendid debut at the Paris Salon of 1953. At the end of the year this model was put on the market at an absurdly low price (considering its performance) of $6,800. The production of this model totaled about 100 units.

In 1955 the 550 Spyder developed into the 550 Spyder-RS. This new model, influenced by the Lotus, had a completely new frame with small-diameter steel tubes, and it weighed 89 pounds less than the 550 of the previous years. Its dry weight was 1,213 pounds. Even when the 23.7 gallon fuel tank and the 8-1/2 quart oil tank were filled, the car weighed only 1,510 pounds. As for the tire sizes, the front tires measured 5.00-16 and the rear 5.25-16. The maximum speed was 137 mph, and the time required for the standing start 1/4 mile was about 16 seconds.

In 1957 the RS model was further refined and developed into the RSK Type 718. The chassis was made both lighter and lower, and the suspensions were improved greatly. Incidentally, the "K" of the "RSK" was derived from the fact that the carrier tubes of the front suspension resembled a letter K on a plan view drawing. Reflecting plans in progress at the time for developing a Formula II car, the steering box was placed in the center of the chassis, and ball joints were adopted for the first time to replace the king pins. The rear suspension was improved with low, single-pivot swing axles and torsion bars, after the Mercedes style. The output of the 1,498-cc engine was gradually increased, and that of the RSK fitted with two Weber carburetors was said to produce 148 HP/8,400 rpm. The vogue in those days was to attach to the tail of the car a pair of vertical fins, like those on airplanes, in order to increase directional stability at high speeds, and the RSK, likewise, was provided with two small tail fins.

The years from 1954 to 1959, when the RS Spyder and the RSK were active in racing competition, was also the period when big cars like Ferrari, Aston Martin, Jaguar, Lotus, Maserati, and OSCA were competing with all their might and staging very spectacular sports car races. Against these vehicles with nearly twice the displacement, the Porsche cars prov-

Type 550, which made a debut at Le Mans in 1953

550 Spyder

Four-camshaft engine mounted in a midship position of the 550 Spyder

ed formidable. Porsche's racing teams, led by von Hanstein, included such ace drivers as Herrmann, Barth, Paul Frere, Frankenberg, Jean Behra, and von Trips (many of whom were the last of the amateurs maintaining the traditions of "gentlemen drivers"). There is not space here to enumerate all the brilliant results achieved by the RS and RSK cars with such drivers, but mention should be made of the fact that at Le Mans in 1955, Polensky/Frankenberg placed fourth in the overall classification; in 1956, Frankenberg/von Trips took fifth place; and in 1958, the three cars with Behra/Herrmann, Barth/Frere, and Beaufort/Linge captured the third, fourth, and fifth places.

In 1960, with a big improvement in its suspension, the RS developed into the RS-60. The swing axles in the rear suspension were finally eliminated, and double wishbones and double-joint driveshafts were adopted. As a result, handling was greatly improved. The engine was of two types: 1,498 cc (85 x 66 mm), 150 HP/7,800 rpm and 1,588 cc (88 x 66 mm), 160 HP/7,800 rpm. For competition that year, Porsche entered the new RS-60 and the RSK of the previous year. Besides winning the championship with an RS-60 (Bonnier/Herrmann) at the Targa Florio, Porsche placed second and fourth in the 1,000 km race at Nürburgring, and took the second place behind Ferrari, who captured the sportscar constructors' championship for the year.

The 1961 model, called the RS-61, had small, detailed chassis improvements, and was fitted with one of the following four types of Flat-4 DOHC engines: 1,588 cc, 1,606 cc, 1,679 cc, or 1,967 cc. The body was of two styles: the traditional open Spyder, or a coupé with an odd, angular roof (which foreshadowed that of the 904 of later years). Four units of this model participated in the Le Mans race of the same year. The results were: fifth place by the 2-liter open vehicle, seventh place by the 1,606-cc coupé, and tenth place by the 1,588-cc coupé. Of the RS-61 Spyders that were particularly active in 1961, one had a longer wheelbase than the others. This was explained the following year by the appearance of the GT prototype with a Flat-8 engine.

550 Spyder, with Herrmann and Linge, which wo

the 1,500-cc class at the Mille Miglia in 1954

As will be mentioned later, Porsche took part in Formula II races from 1957 to 1960 and obtained good results. In 1961, when Formula I was reduced to 1.5 liters, it became possible for Porsche to enter its existing Formula II cars, without any modification, in Formula I races. However, specially for this purpose, the Flat-8 1.5-liter engine was soon developed. The 2-liter type based on it was fitted in the GT prototype of the RS series. Incidentally, from 1962 onward, the sports-car constructors' championship was awarded, not to the

65

Engine of the
550/1500 RS

Opened-up view of the 550/1500 RS, showing the 4-camshaft engine placed in front of the rear axle

550/1500 RS Spyder
A limited number of this model was produced in 1955 and 1956. Many of them were imported to the United States and were active in sports car racing.

Cockpit of the 550/1500 RS

67

71

718/1500 RSK Spyder, 1958—1959
It had vertical tail fins for forward stability.

72

Front of the above car
Notice the nose with a hatch for the spare tire, which in the 550 RS used to be stored inside the engine cover.

RSK with Jean Behra at the Goodwood GT race in 1958

sole winner in overall classifications, but to the winner in each of the three classes of vehicles: of 1,000 cc or less, 2,500 cc or less, and 4,000 or less, each of which was to be a GT prototype. This new ruling was of great advantage to Porsche, whose cars, up to that time, had to compete with 3-liter Ferraris and Maseratis on equal terms.

The Porsche GT prototype of 1962 was fitted with a Flat-8 1,981-cc (76 x 54.6 mm) engine placed on an RS-60 chassis of 1961. Provided with four double-choke Weber carburetors and a dual ignition system, this engine was said to develop 210 HP. It had a widely different cooling system from that of the former 4-cylinder engines, since a gear-driven nylon fan was placed horizontally above the engine. The gearbox also was a new type with six speeds. As this new engine was used in races before it was fully developed, it often caused trouble. The best results obtained by vehicles fitted with this engine were the third places won by Bonnier/Vaccarella at the Targa Florio and Nürburgring. At Le Mans, old Carrera-Abarth cars fitted with this engine placed seventh and twelfth. In the GT Prototype Class-2 championship race, however, a Porsche with the same engine won by a wide margin from the second-place Alfa Romeo.

In the 1963 model the torsion bars and the double trailing links in the front suspension were eliminated in favor of coils and double wishbones, and the Flat-8 engine had a higher output of 230 HP. The sole highlight for this year was the victory at the Targa Florio of the machine with Bonnier/Abathe driving, which averaged 64 mph. To this might be added the fact that Porsche captured the Class-2 championship.

RS Spyder, 1960

RS 60 which, with Barth/Seidel, placed tenth at Le Mans in 1960

RS 61 Coupé

RS Spyder with a 2-liter Flat-8 engine
This machine, driven by Graham Hill, placed third in the 1,000-km race at Nürburgring in May, 1962

Cars of the Porsche Works team for Le Mans, 1961
The engine capacities were: No.36: 1,588 cc, No.33: 1,967 cc, No.32: 1,606 cc, and No.30: 1,679.

73

79

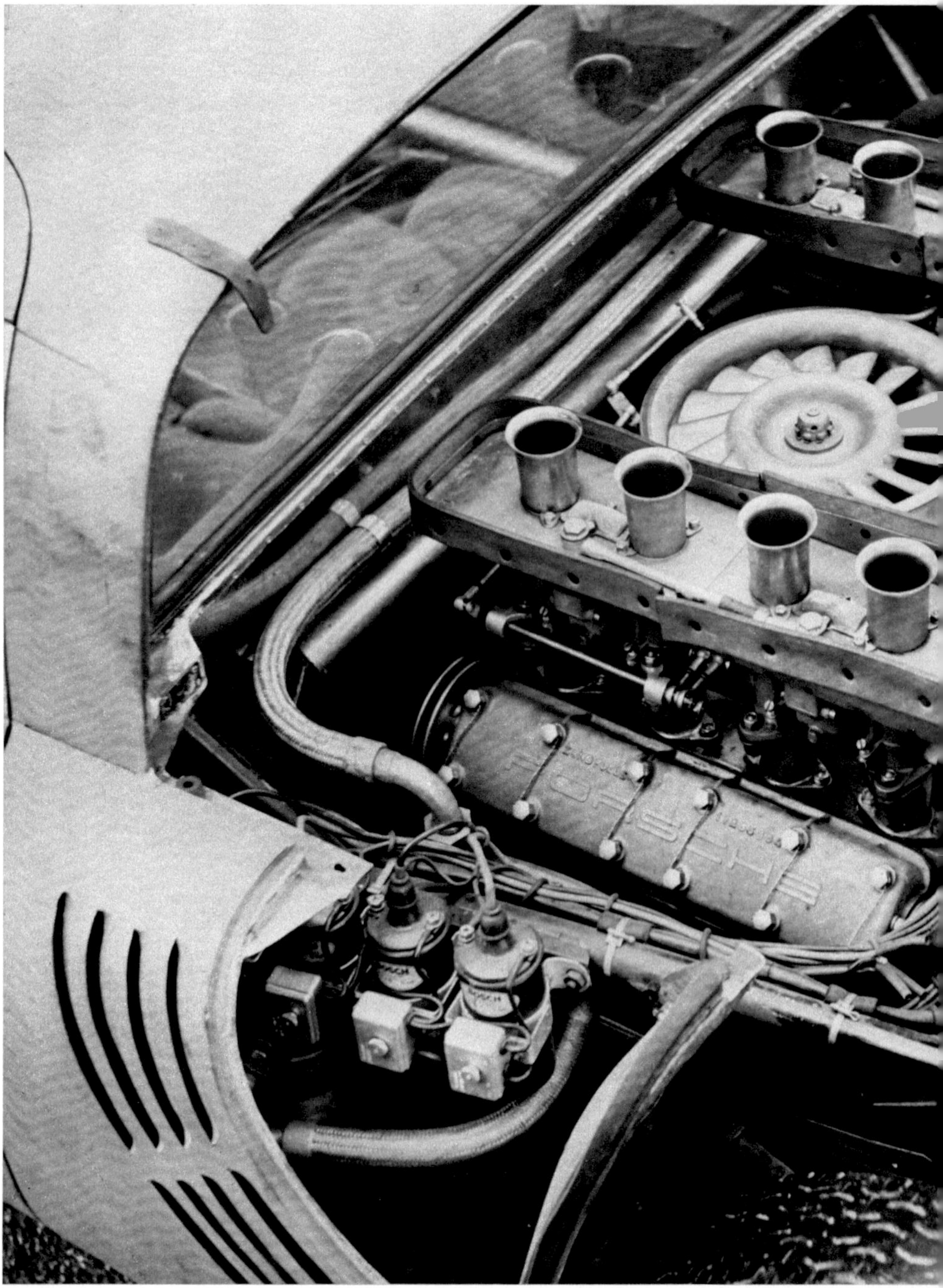

Two-liter Flat-8 engine in the RS Spyder

CHAPTER 4
G.P. Formula Cars, 1957-1962

The year 1957 was marked by the appearance of 1.5-liter Formula II cars in Grand Prix racing. At the German Grand Prix of the same year, they were allowed to race together with 2.5-liter Formula I cars. (This practice has since become a tradition.) Porsche was enthusiastic about participation, not only because it was thoroughly familiar with the Nürburgring, but also because its 1.5-liter cars required only slight modification for participation.
At this Grand Prix, a Porsche RSK Spyder (with the seat shifted to the center of the same body) driven by Barth, defeated a Cooper Climax and won the championship. Encouraged by this success, Porsche next sent a remodeled RSK single-seater to the Formula II race held as a preliminary event to the French Grand Prix of that year. Jean Behra, who drove the Porsche car, won the race by defeating both Stirling Moss in a Cooper and Peter Collins in a Dino Ferrari. He showed that the RSK, though slower through corners than regular G.P. cars, was faster on straightaways because of its aerodynamic body.

Highly elated by these successes, Porsche, the next year, built a regular Formula II machine by using RSK components. Double trailing arms identical to those of the RSK were used at the front, while at the rear, a standard RSK engine was placed on a chassis fitted with torsion bars and double wishbones. The gearbox was a new 6-speed type. This Porsche F-2 machine took part in the Monaco G.P. race, with von Trips at the wheel. Because of its compact body, the car attained faster lap times than McLaren's F-1 Cooper and G. Hill's Lotus, and looked certain to win. Unfortunately, however, the machine skidded on an oil slick on the road and could not finish the race.
A year later, in 1960, Porsche, with even greater hope for success in F-2 racing, allotted a Works car to Bonnier/Hill, lent another car to Stirling Moss of the Rob Walker team, and attempted to make a clean sweep of the F-2 races. Since, in those days, the Cooper, Lotus, and Ferrari F-2 cars were not strong rivals, Porsche won second place at Brussels, first place at Pau, second and fifth places at Solitude, and first, second, and fourth through sixth places at Nürburgring. Thus the championship for F-2 racing for 1960 fell into the hands of Porsche.
In 1961, when Formula I was reduced to 1.5 liters, Porsche decided to go F-1 racing in earnest. For this purpose, 4-cylinder cars of 1960 were used, which had an output of 150 HP/8,000 rpm and a top speed of 161.5 mph. However, despite efforts made by Dan Gurney and Jo Bonnier, the best results Porsche obtained were second places taken by Gurney at the French and U.S. Grand Prix.
In 1962, Porsche concentrated all its efforts on Grand Prix racing—so much so that interest in sports car racing was somewhat neglected—and produced a Flat-8 F-1 machine. It had a 4-camshaft

Flat-8 Formula I car which, driven by Dan Gurney, won the French Grand Prix at Rouen in 1962

Ferry Porsche and Dan Gurney, who is explaining the condition of his machine to the chief mechanic

77

Final-development model of the Porsche Formula I machine, which appeared in the 1962 season

1,494.4-cc (66 x 54.6 mm) engine with a compression ratio of 10:1. Provided with four Weber carburetors, it had an output of 180 HP/9,200 rpm and a torque of 109.9 lb.ft./7,200 rpm. Instead of coils, with their high wind resistance, torsion bars were again adopted in both the front and rear suspensions, and double wishbones were used both front and rear. The brakes were discs made by Porsche. After efforts to make the car as slim and compact as possible, the body width was reduced from 36.2 inches of the 1961 4-cylinder model to 31.8 inches, and the car's weight was reduced from 1,036 pounds to 996 pounds. However, owing to its horizontally opposed engine, the body was still larger than those of the Lotus and the BRM.

This was the year when the old 4-cylinder Lotus Climax piloted by Stirling Moss, the Lotus with a new V-8 engine driven by Jim Clark, and the V-6 Ferrari were beginning to show their true worth, so that Porsche cars for the first time were forced to accept a subordinate position in racing. The only consolation was that the Porsche F-1 driven by Dan Gurney won the French Grand Prix. After this year, Porsche retired from Grand Prix racing and concentrated its efforts on GT/Prototype racing.

Flat-8 1,494.4-cc (66 x 54.6 mm) engine of the above car (David Phipps photo)

Comparison of the '62 8-cylinder car (above) and the '61 4-cylinder car
The 4-cylinder car had many parts common with the RSK sports car, but the 8-cylinder car was of completely new design.

CHAPTER 5
The 911/912 and the 914

911

The 911, which made its debut at the Frankfurt Show in the fall of 1963, was the first completely new model built after the 356 was introduced fifteen years before. At the time of its debut, this 6-cylinder model was called the 901, but the name was changed to 911 when it was put on the market. The reason was that Peugeot had registered internationally for its exclusive use as type numbers all the three-digit numbers with a zero in the middle. The company reserved this right for passenger cars only, not for racing cars. The 911 was a completely new design from bumper to bumper, and it had no parts common with the 356 C/SC that preceded it. Comparison of dimensions and engine specifications are as follows:

	911	356 SC
Wheelbase	87 inches	82.7 inches
Tread (front)	52.6 inches	51.4 inches
Tread (rear)	51.9 inches	50 inches
Overall length	163.9 inches	157.9 inches
Overall width	63.3 inches	65.7 inches
Overall height	52 inches	51.8 inches
Weight (DIN)	2,381 lbs.	2,062 lbs.
Engine type	6-cylinder SOHC	4-cylinder OHV
Displacement	1,991 cc	1,582 cc
Output	130 HP/ 6,100 rpm	95 HP/ 5,800 rpm

As can be seen from the above, both the wheelbase and the overall length of the 911 were greater than those of the 356 C/SC, but its body width was 2.4 inches narrower. The original design objective of the 911 was a two-plus-two GT car with the same high performance and riding comfort as the 356. But in view of the large changes that had occurred in customers' demands and in road and traffic conditions since the time the 356 had been planned, a completely new design approach was made. In order to have larger window areas and still obtain the necessary high strength and rigidity, the monocoque structure was further refined.

Another change appeared in the 6-cylinder engine of the 911. To meet the performance required, the existing OHV 4-cylinder engine was no longer adequate; and to adopt a 4-camshaft, 4-cylinder engine like that of the Carrera would have been too costly. Accordingly, a single OHC, 6-cylinder horizontally opposed engine was selected. It was a 1,991-cc (80 x 66 mm) oversquare type, with the crankshaft supported by eight main bearings; and the camshaft of each bank was driven by a double roller chain from a countershaft connected to the crankshaft through a flat gear. This made the 911 the first Porsche car to have a chain drive for the camshaft. As for carburetors, a Solex 40 PI triple choke type was used for each bank. This system gave an output of 130 HP/6,100 rpm, with a torque of 75 lb.ft./4,300 rpm.

A 5-speed gearbox was used for the first time in this production model. The suspension systems were also entirely different from those of the 356 series.

First model 911, with 356 C/SC models in the background

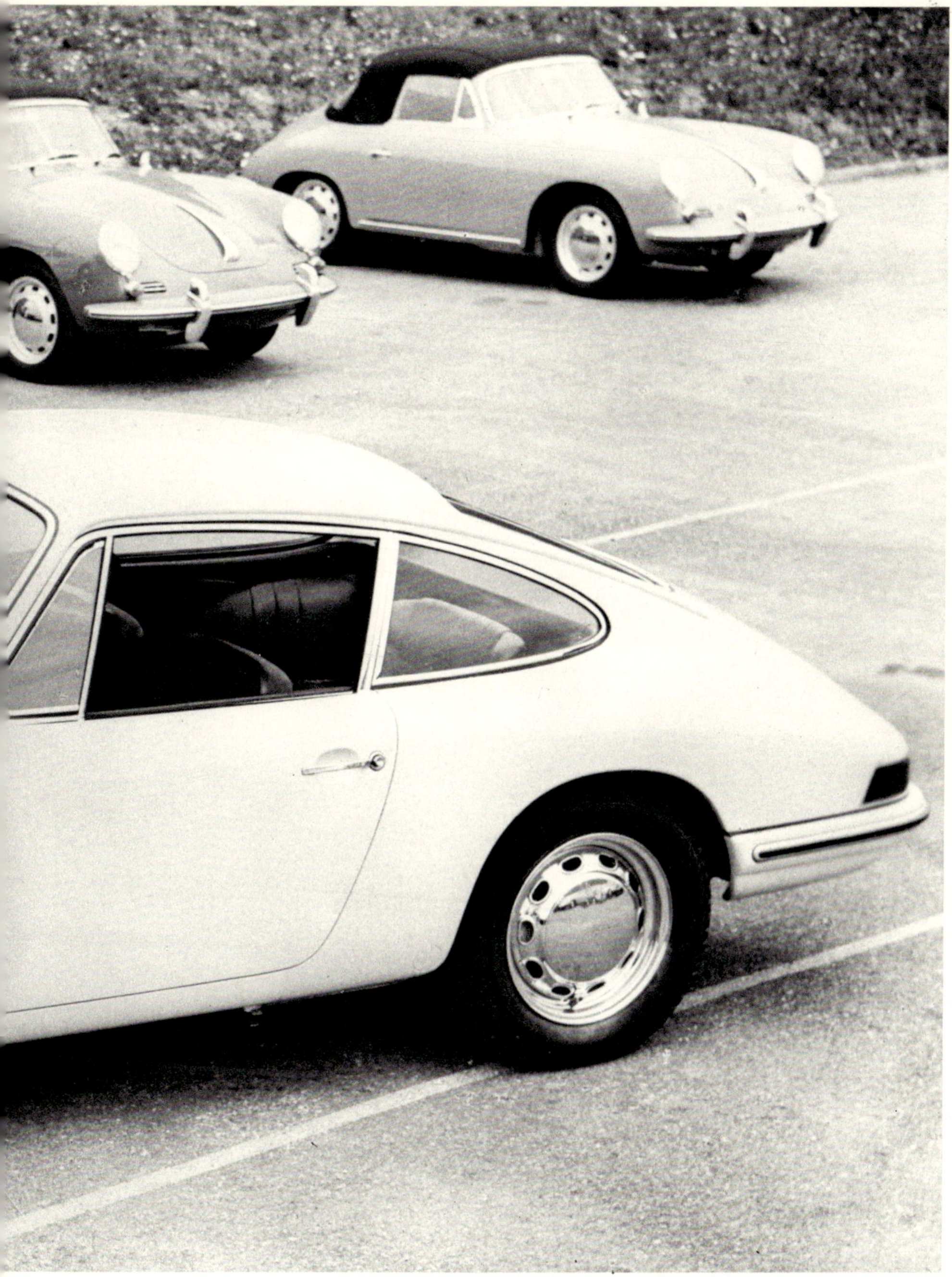

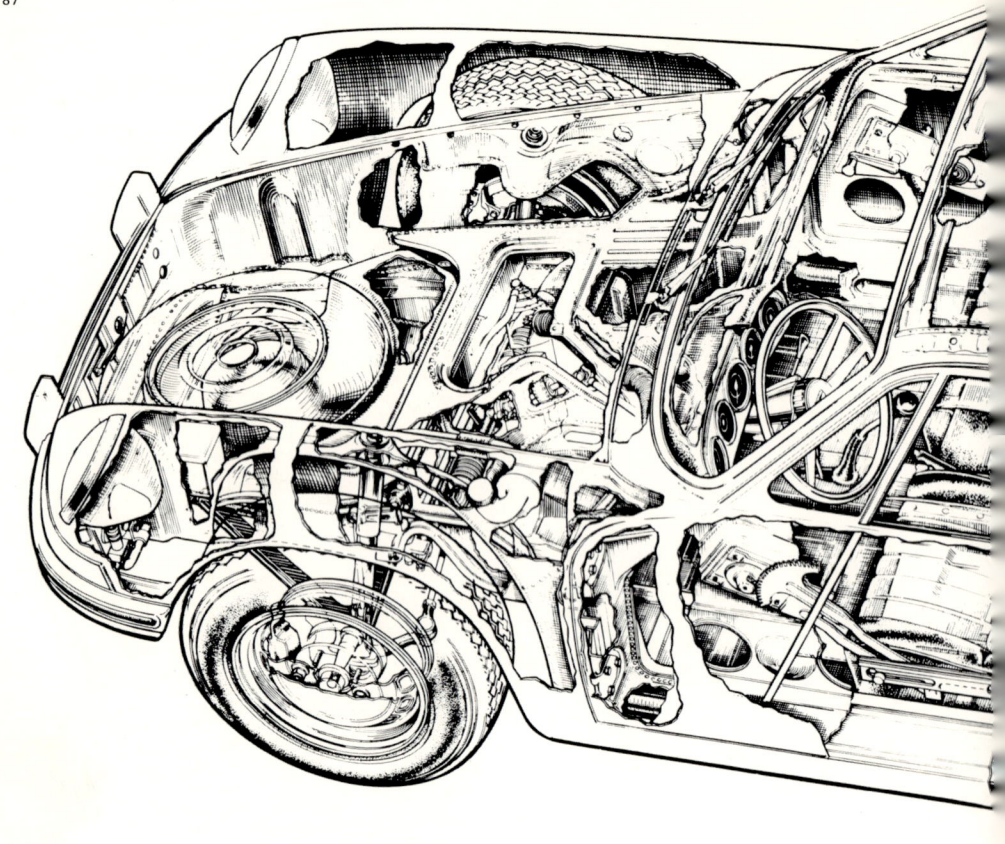

Cutaway drawing of the 911, showing Porsche's first monocoque body

The front system consisted of MacPherson struts and longitudinal torsion bars acting on the lower control arms. The system at the rear was composed of a trailing A arm and a double-joint driveshaft, with transverse torsion bars carrying the load. A ZF rack-and-pinion type steering gear was used because of its safety in case of a collision, and because of good space utilization. The adoption of the Macpherson suspension system also allowed a large trunk space, which was more fully achieved by burying the spare tire in the floor.

The brakes were Dunlop type discs made by ATE, which measured 9.3/9.6 in. in diameter, and the rear system contained small-diameter drums for handbraking. The wheels remained 15" x 4-1/2 J, and the tires were 165 HR 15. As for the performance, the maximum speed was 130 mph and the time for

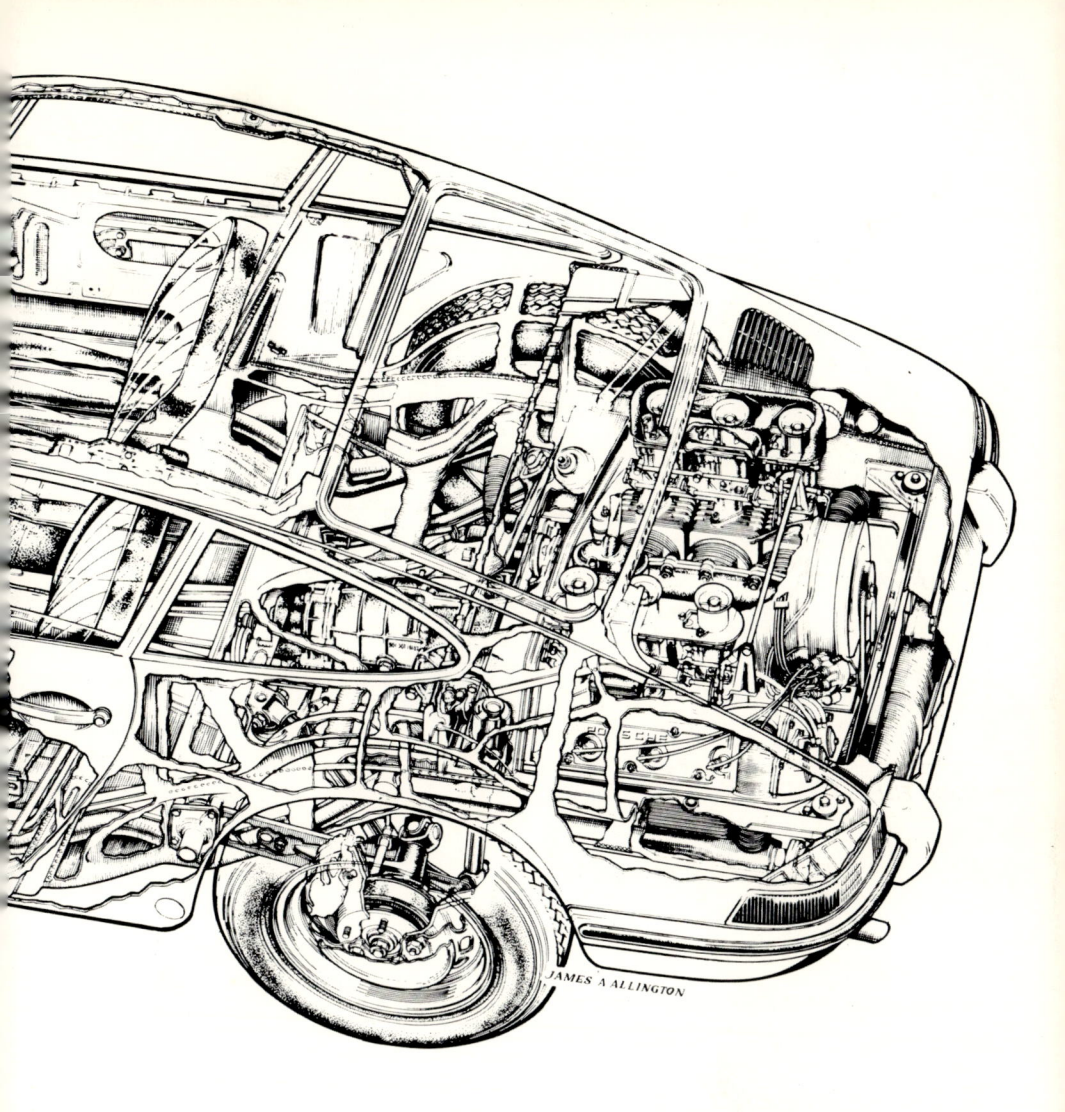

0–400 meters was 16.5 seconds, both of which greatly bettered those of the 356 SC.

In the United States the 911 was an expensive car, selling at $7,500. Its lower-priced version, the model 912, fitted with an engine from the 356 SC (4-cylinder OHV, 1,582 cc, 90 HP/5,800 rpm), was also put on the market at $5,095. Except for its 4-speed gearbox (a 5-speed was an option), this model was similar to the 911, and had a top speed of 115 mph and a 0–400 meters time of 18.2 seconds. Great improvements were noted in the handling of the 911/912, as the tendency toward the sudden change to oversteer, due to the swing axle of the 356 series, was completely eliminated, leaving only neutral steer or slight understeer.

In 1967, several variations of the 911 were produced. First of all, the 130-HP

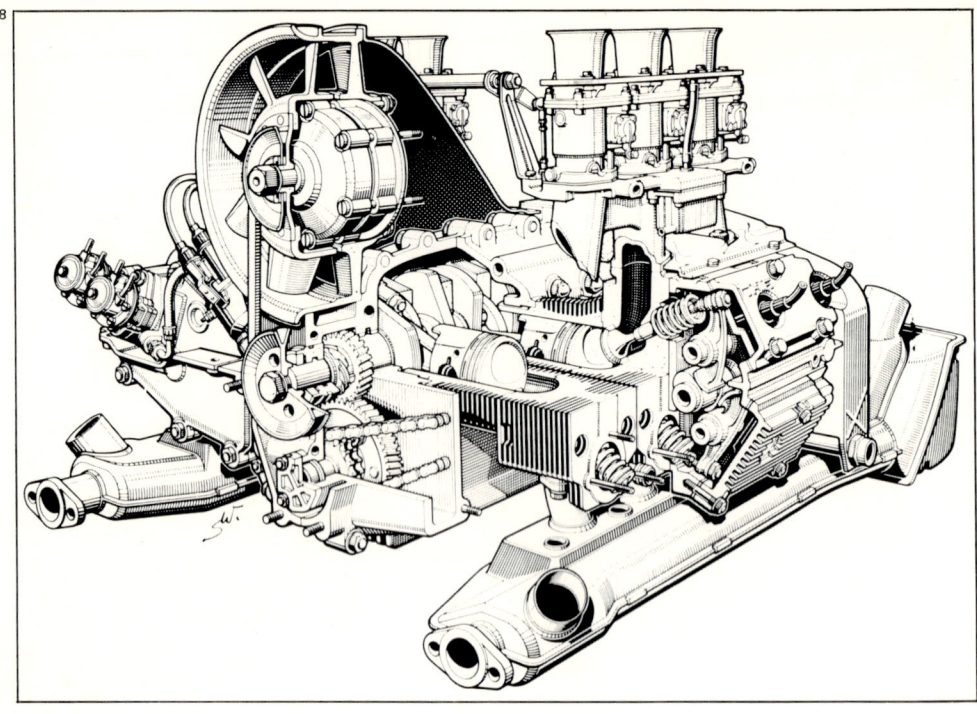

SOHC Flat-6 engine of the 911

911 became the 911 L, and below it appeared the touring type 911 T with a 110 HP/5,800 rpm (8.6:1 compression) engine and a 4 speed gearbox. Moreover, as a high-performance version, the 911 S, with a 160 HP/6,600 rpm (9.9:1 compression) engine and 6 J x 15 light-alloy wheels was added to the line. (Compared to the former steel-plate wheels weighing 41.6 lbs., these new aluminum alloy wheels weighed only 11.7 lbs., though they cost about five times as much.) As for the bodywork, a new style with a removable hardtop called the "Targa" was offered.

Another creation was an automatic clutch system called the "Sportmatic," that became an optional item for the entire 911 line—a very interesting feature reflecting a new trend of the times. This was not a so-called automatic transmission device, but rather a combination of a 4-speed gearbox and a torque converter/plate clutch. When the hand touched the gear lever, an electromagnetic switch became activated to release the clutch, allowing manual gear shifting as if the gearbox were of a conventional type. When the throttle was opened, the torque converter trans-

Six-cylinder engine mounted on the chassis of the 911 S, 1967 – 1968

mitted power; and at 3,500 rpm, the clutch engaged directly to operate in the conventional manner. In other words, this system was intermediate between a conventional and an automatic clutch system, and there was practically no power loss.

Beginning with the 1969 model, the 911 had two new variations: the 911 E and the 911 S, both of which had mechanical fuel injection equipment. Their outputs were increased to 140 HP/6,500 rpm and 170 HP/6,800 rpm, and the maximum speeds also were raised to 134 mph and 140 mph. The wheelbase was increased by 2.2 in. and became 89.2 in. This was to make the weight distribution further approach the ideal value — the former 40/60 distribution was improved to 42/58. As a result, both straightline stability and cornering performance are said to have improved.

As for the suspension system, another change made was the replacement of the front torsion bars of the 911 E with hydro-pneumatic struts made by Boge (which were also optional on the 911 T and 911 S). The oil and gas in these struts sustained the load, and performed a self-leveling action whenever they were

Model 912, 1965, a lower-price version of the 911

compressed. This leveling action was due to the resulting pumping action and served to quickly return the car to its proper position.

In 1970, the engines of all models of the 911 series had the cylinder bore enlarged by 4 mm, and their capacity became 2,195 cc. The outputs of the 911 T (with carburetors), the 911 E (with fuel injection), and the 911 S (with fuel injection) were 125 HP/5,800 rpm, 155 HP/6,200 rpm, and 180 HP/6,500 rpm, respectively. As for the performance of the 911 S, the maximum speed, with an increase of 3 mph. became 143 mph., and the time for the 0–100 km/h. speed (62 mph.) was improved to 7.2 seconds. With these improvements, production of the 4–cylinder 912 was discontinued.

The racing model of the 911 series was the 911 R. Its engine was the fuel injection S type, with the compression ratio further raised to 10.3:1 to develop 210 HP. Its body, except for the doors and the front fenders, was of FRP (Fiberglass-Reinforced Plastic), and the door windows and the rear window were of plexiglas. The car's weight was only 1,764 pounds, which was 507 pounds less than that of the 911 S.

The 911 and its variations were, from the beginning, looked upon as promising rally machines. When Vic Elford and Björn Waldegaard joined the Porsche Works teams, they suddenly began to attract public attention. The teams chose, rather than the 911 S, the more lightweight 911 T, and had some units fitted out as rally cars. With these the

Model 911 S, 1967
This is a high-performance version of the 911, with the output raised to 160 HP. It was fitted with 6J x 15 aluminium alloy wheels.

Dashboard of the 911 S, produced up to 1969
Beginning with the 1970 model, crash pads were attached — even to the horn button on the steering wheel.

911 Targa

Fuel injected engine of the 911 E/S

911 S Targa, 1970

*911 R: a racing model with a 911 S fuel injection engine tuned for 210 HP
This car participated in the '69 Tour de France.*

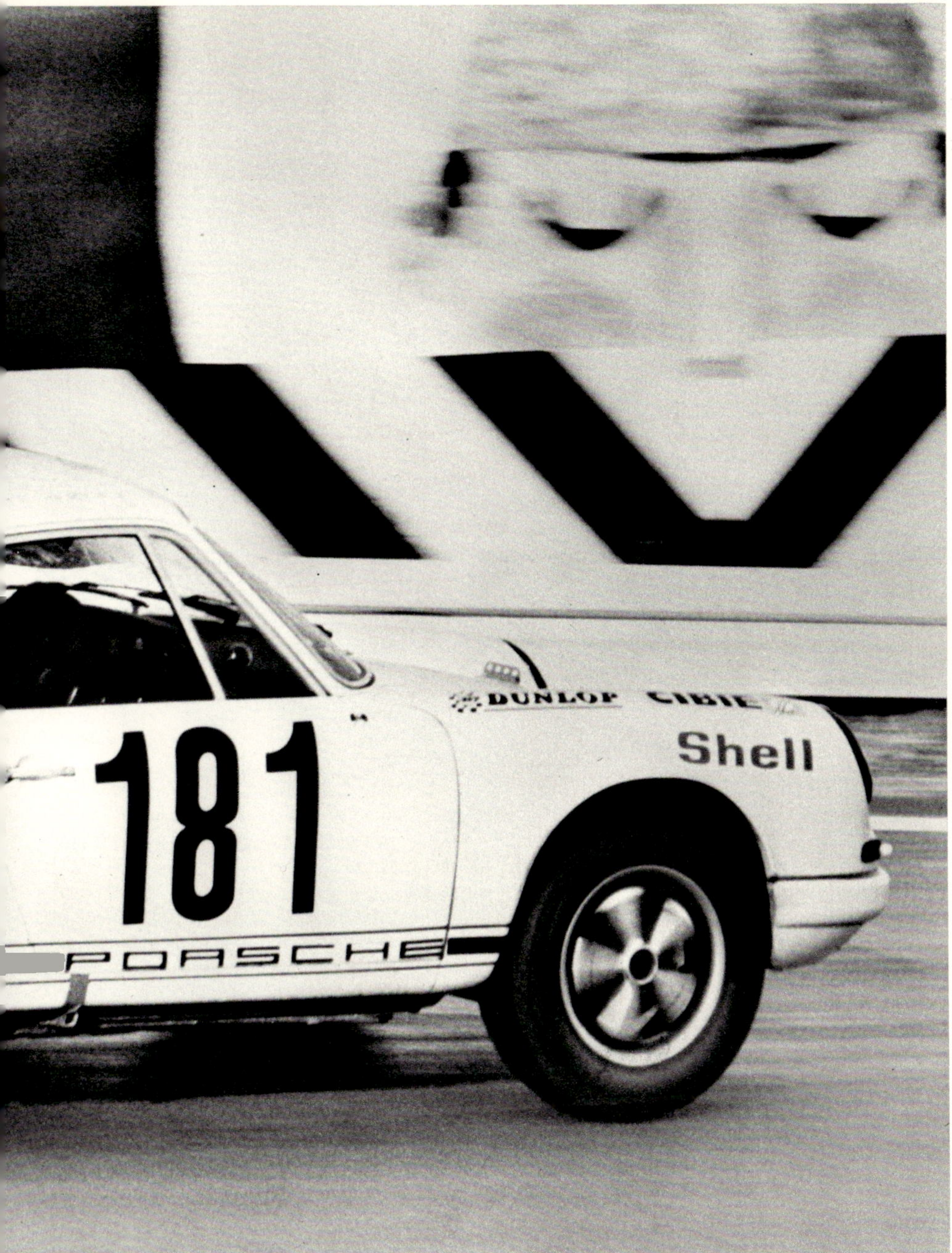
DUNLOP
CIBIE
Shell
181
PORSCHE

911 S that won the '70 Monte Carlo Rally

teams devoted their energies to the Monte Carlo Rally, which was reputed to be one of the most colorful rallies and with the highest publicity value. In this rally, in 1967, Elford placed third; in 1968, Elford and Toivonen placed first and second. In 1969, Waldegaard, with the 911 S, became the victor; and in 1970, Wadegaard and Larrousse driving their 2.2-liter 911 S machines, captured the first and second places. Thus Porsche established an unprecedented record of three years' successive victories at Monte Carlo.

In the meantime, the 911 obtained homologation in 1967 as a Group-2 Touring Car and began to participate in touring-car races in Europe. Its victory in the 24-hour race at Spa in 1967 was just one example of its performance. In 1968, however, the BMW 2002 TI with fuel injection was found to be somewhat faster, and there were cases where some drivers of the 911 replaced their engines with dual ignition Carrera-6 engines.

Here we might entertain a supposition to illustrate that automotive engineering techniques are making constant progress — that is, if the 911 had participated in the 1956 German Grand Prix race at Nürburgring, it would have defeated the Mercedes W 196 Formula I machine driven by Fangio. This assumption is based on the fact that, against the fastest lap of 9 min. 41 sec. (a new record established in the race by Fangio's machine), the best lap of the 911, a pure production model, was 9 min. 36 sec.

914 and 914/6

The center of attraction at the 1969 Frankfurt Show were the completely new mid-engine GT cars called the VW-Porsche 914 and 914/6, which had been developed through close cooperation between Porsche and Volkswagen. Perhaps it was natural for Porsche, with their long experience with midship engine racing cars since the 1952 Model 550 Spyder, to use the same layout for highly practical GT cars that would be produced in quantity in the 1970s.

Porsche designed the 914 series, while Volkswagen, the world's fourth largest automobile manufacturer, supplied the VW 411 E fuel-injection engines as well as the bodies. Furthermore, the VW-Porsche AG, which was created through equal investments by the two companies, was placed in charge of sales of the 914 series.

There are two different cars in the 914 series, differing basically in the engine. The 914 has the VW 411 E 4-cylinder OHV, 1,670-cc, 80 HP/4,900 rpm engine with electronically controlled fuel injection. The 914/6 has the 6-cylinder SOHC, 1,991-cc, 110 HP/5,800 rpm engine with two triple throat Weber carburetors; the same engine used for the 911 T through 1969.

Both types have an all-synchromesh 5-speed gearbox, with gear ratios varying somewhat according to the engine output and characteristics. As with the 911, the "Sportmatic," a 4-speed gearbox plus a torque converter, is optional.

The two types have an identical body, being an open-type monocoque of all welded steel plates, with side sills and scuttles as main structures. An important feature is the use of quarter panels serving also as roll bars, which, as in the Targa, turns the car into an open style when the lightweight top made of FRP is removed. Hence the same unit serves both as a coupé and a cabriolet. The engine is mounted differently than that of the 911 — the engine being in front of the rear axle with the clutch side facing the rear. This layout makes the car definitely a two-seater, not a two-plus-two seater, as was the case with earlier Porsche production models. The same layout has also resulted in wide trunk spaces both in the front and in the rear, which can serve as crush areas in case of an accident.

As with the 911, the front suspension system consists of Macpherson struts and longitudinal torsion bars, which act on lower transverse links. The system at the rear, unlike that in older models, has thick semi-trailing arms, made of welded steel plates, and coil damper units. The wheels are all fitted with disc brakes, but without a servomechanism. The disc sizes are different in the two types of cars, being 9.1 in./9.4 in. in diameter for the 914, and 9.2 in./9.4 in. in diameter for the 914/6. The front discs for the 914/6 have ventilating holes. The steering is ZF rack-and-pinion type with a 17.78:1 ratio. The tire sizes for the 4-cylinder

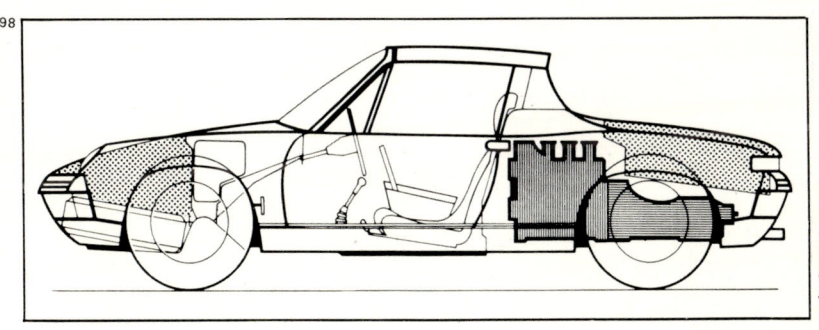

Cross sectional view of the 914/6. Notice the large trunk space in the front and rear.

914/6 making its debut at the '69 Frankfurt Show

4 0 Liter Kofferraum

Production model of the 914/6

Low-priced version of the 914
This car has a VW411 E, 1.7-liter, fuel injected engine.

102

Cockpit of the 914/6

103

914's engine (4-cylinder, OHV, 1.7-liter, with electronically controlled fuel injection) and the 5-speed transmission

914/6 at '70 Le Mans for its first participation

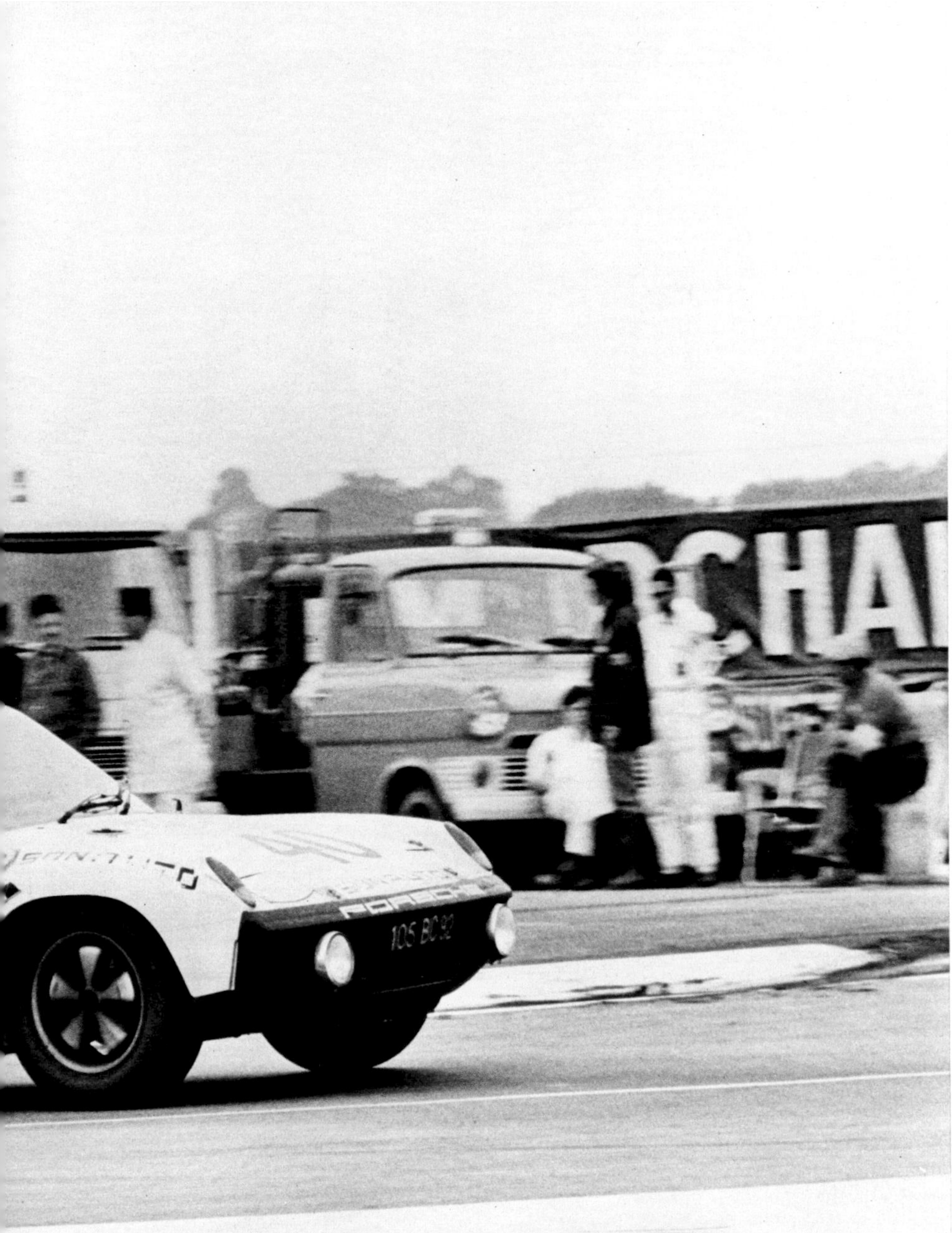
PORSCHE
105 BC 92

914 rally car

type are 4½J J rim with 155 SR 15, and those for the 6-cylinder type are 5½ J rim with 165 HP 15. The car's weight is relatively heavy — 1,984 pounds for the 914, and 2,072 pounds for the 914/6.

The performance of the 914 and the 914/6 is contrasted as follows: (maximum speed) 108 mph and 124 mph; (0—100 km/h) 13.0 sec. and 9.9 sec. As for their power performance, even the faster type 914/6 comes between the 2-liter 911 T and the 2.2-liter 911 T. But the excellent maneuverability of the two types is closer to that of a racing car than is any other regularly produced automobile. Because of the midship layout (with large masses like the engine and riders placed near the center of gravity), the steering response is very sensitive, and both types can maintain ideal neutral steer up to high speeds.

Unlike those of a racing car, however, the front and rear tires are, for practical reasons, of the same size. This fact, together with the characteristics of the radial tires, gives both types of cars a tendency to breakaway suddenly during extreme cornering. And unless the driver is well accustomed to the car, it is difficult for him to predict this characteristic.

Nevertheless, both types have an unbelievably roomy interior and provide good visibility for midship GT cars. Accordingly, the two types, especially the 914 with a flexible 4-cylinder engine, can serve for shopping purposes and high-speed touring — ideal cars for young couples desiring both features. They are priced much lower than other Porsche cars preceding them. Incidentally, at Le Mans '70, a practically stock 914/6 captured the GT class title with an average speed of 98.4 mph.

CHAPTER 6
Racing Models since the 904

Carrera GTS 904

It was back in November, 1963, that Porsche made public an epoch-making GT racing car — the mid-engine Carrera GTS 904. This car replaced the Carrera 2000 GS, which was based on the 356, and which, up to that time, had represented Porsche in GT class races. The 904 was in many respects a great improvement over the earlier Porsches. To begin with, it was the first production model with a midship engine, and its body was made of lightweight FRP.

Though its engine (Type 587/3) was based on the 4-cylinder, 4-camshaft, 1,966-cc (92 x 74 mm) engine for the racing-type RS and Carrera 2, it had undergone great improvements. Much consideration was especially given to its cooling system, resulting in enlargement of the oil cooler and an increase in the width of the cooling fins of the light-alloy cylinders (with ferral-treated cylinder walls) from 7 mm to 20 mm. The output was raised to 180 HP/7,200 rpm with a compression ratio of 9.8:1, by using two triple-throat carburetors and extreme valve timings of 79°–93°–88°–60°. There was also a less powerful 155HP/6900 rpm engine for use in a "town" car. The chassis was composed of box-frame side rails measuring 7.8 in. in depth, which were made of strong steel plates welded together, and cross members at the front, center, and rear. The FRP body, built by Heinkel, which was famous for its aircraft, was firmly attached to the chassis with bolts and adhesive agents, giving the structure a very high overall strength.

As for the suspension, experience gained in constructing Formula machines was utilized. The front suspension consisted of double wishbones and coils, while the rear suspension had upper and lower reverse "A" arms of equal length and upper and lower parallel radius arms. The upper radius arm was somewhat shorter, to produce a certain amount of rear-axle steering effect.

Large wheels 15" in diameter were still used, for, according to Porsche, the 904 was not a so-called "airport racer," but a machine designed for racing on all types of road surfaces — especially over courses like Targa Florio. The standard tires for both the front and rear were 165HR15, Dunlop-SP DB59, but optional racing-type 5.50L 15, R6D12 tires were available. The dry weight of the car was only 1,267 pounds, and even when 29 gallons of fuel and 10 quarts of oil were added, the car was still 331 pounds lighter than the existing Carrera 2000 GS.

In those days, the minimum production required for the GT category was 100 units per year. Porsche produced that number of units in less than six months and obtained its GT homologation. They were marketed at a remarkably low price of DM29,700 (about $8,060).

During the '64 and '65 seasons a considerable number of 904s were raced by both Works teams and private teams. At Le Mans, Nürburgring, and Sebring, among others, the 904 was overshadowed by fierce competition between the Ford GT and the Ferrari 275/P. But

106

107

904 which was made public for the first time in November, 1963 (top and left)

108

Sturdy frme of the 904

904 participating in the '65 Monte Carlo Rally

904

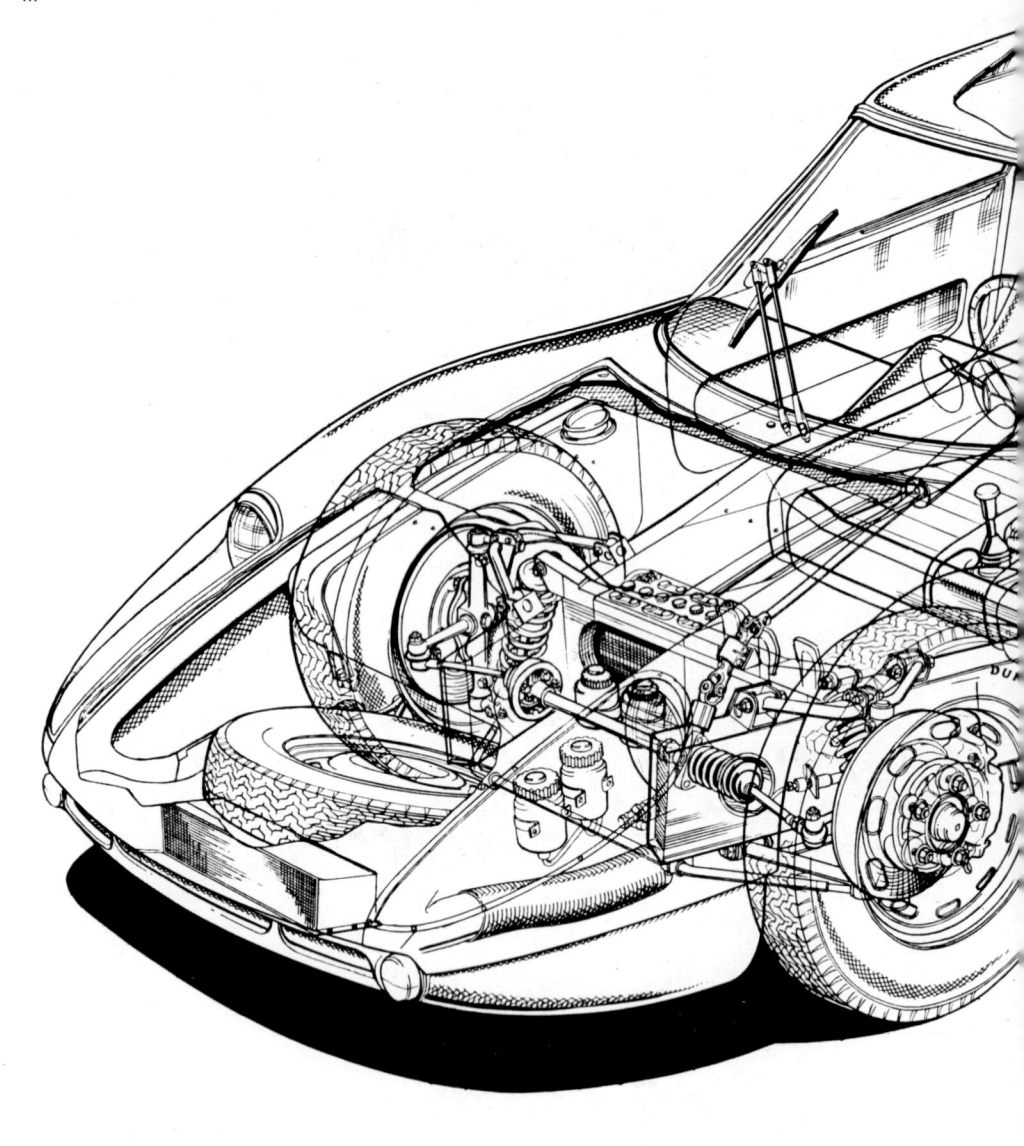

Structural drawing of the 904

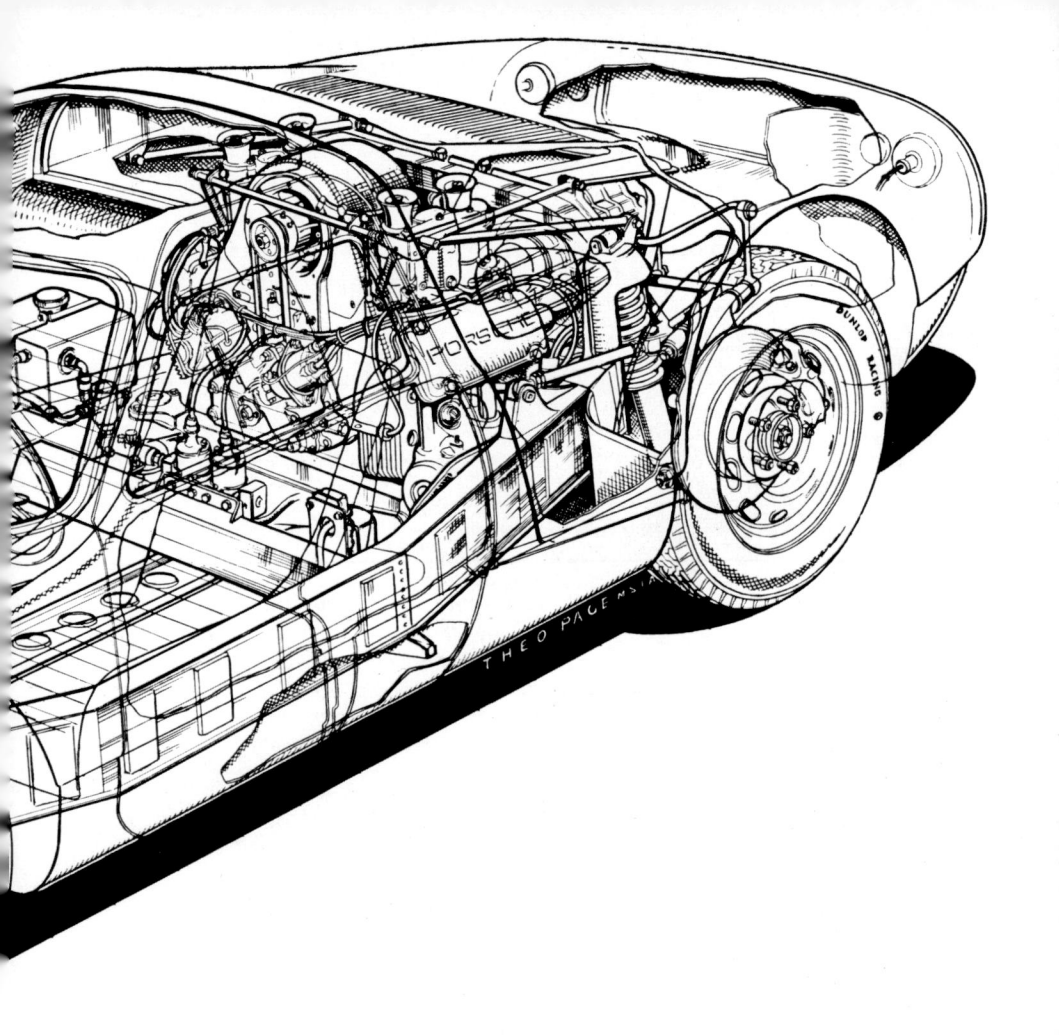

at the Targa Florio, traditionally Porsche's favorite arena, it captured the first and second places in its debut year of 1964. In the following year, even at Le Mans, the 904, with Linge/Böhringer, not only finished in the upper rank in the overall classification, but also won the performance index award. One may say, however, that the high reliability and practicability of this model was demonstrated most prominently when a unit driven by Göhringer won second place in the overall classification at the '65 Monte Carlo Rally. True, the 904 was definitely not an "airport racer."

906 (Carrera 6)

The 906 (Carrera 6), which appeared in 1966, was, one might say, almost as different from the earlier 904 as a racing car is from a sedan. The 904 could have been practical on public roads if piloted by an experienced and patient driver, but the 906 was a pure racing-sports car. In 1966, the FIA rules were revised, and the minimum production per year for Group-4 cars became 50 units. Porsche produced 50 units of the 906 by May of the same year, marketed them at $12,000, and thus obtained FIA's homologation.

The chassis of the 906, which was entirely different from that of the 904, was a multi-steel-tube space frame. The front suspension consisted of double wishbones and coil spring units, and the rear suspension, too, was a double wishbone type. The body was of FRP, and because of the space-frame structure, it had gull-wing type doors.

The 906 was fitted with a 6-cylinder, SOHC, 1,911-cc engine from the production type 911, but with two Weber 46 IDA3C carburetors and a hot cam, it was tuned for 210 HP/8,000 rpm. It

906 "Carrera 6" of 1966

906 with gull-wing type doors

was an exceptionally flexible engine for racing use and was said to have a wide power band of 3,500–8,200 rpm. Beginning with the 1966 Nürburgring 1,000-km race, the car had an alternative engine, in which the Weber carburetors were replaced with a Bosch port-type mechanical fuel injection system. This latter engine had a higher output of 220 HP/8,000 rpm.

The car's weight was light at 1,323 pounds, and the maximum speed was about 168 mph. In the latter half of the year, there appeared also a machine with an 8-cylinder, 4-camshaft, 2.2-liter, 250 HP engine fitted in an identical body. This machine, called the 906/8, developed into the 907 the following year.

It was only during the 1966 season that the 906 served as the chief racing machines of the Works teams, but in that short period they scored a number of wins. After their victory at the Targa Florio, four out of the six units that participated in the Le Mans race placed fourth through seventh, overwhelming the rival Ferrari-Dino 206. Moreover, the 906 captured the championship for the 2-liter sports-car class.

906 LM, 1966

Six-cylinder, 2-liter engine of the 906 LM, which entered the Le Mans '66

109

910 (Carrera 10)

Porsche's Works cars for the 1967 season centered around the 910, which made a debut in the 24-hour race at Daytona Beach. This vehicle was basically the same as the 906, but it had a somewhat different chassis. The rear suspension had four links of the Formula I type, instead of double reverse "A" arms as in the 906, and 13" diameter cast magnesium wheels were used for the first time.

The body resembled that of the 906, but its nose was made both lower and more pointed, so it did not require a nose spoiler as on the 906. The doors, which were not the gull-wing type, opened obliquely to the front. The engine was identical to that of the later model of the 906 — namely, fuel injection type, 1,991-cc. 210 HP/8,000 rpm. But after Targa Florio, there also appeared a model with a flat-8, 2,195-cc. 270 HP/8,600 rpm engine. The wheelbase and the overall length were the same as those of the 906, but the car's height was made still lower and the weight decreased. The top speed was 174 mph.

910, 1967–'68

910 "Berg": a hill climbing racer based on the 910

The two 910s that placed first and third in the '67 Nürburgring 1,000-km race

Extremely simple cockpit of the 910 "Berg"

111

907

Strangely enough, the 907, which had a lower type number, was a later model than the 910. Its first appearance was in April, 1967, on the customary Le Mans Test Day.

The chassis of the 907, except for small details, was the same as that of the 910. The same holds true of the engine, since either a 6-cylinder, 2-liter engine or an 8-cylinder, 2.2-liter engine could be mounted, as in the case of the 910. The body, however, was of completely new design. It came into being through exhaustive research conducted during the winter of 1966 — 67, and was the ultimate in aerodynamic design.

Having been designed with Le Mans as the prime consideration, the 907 was a "Langheck" (Long-tail) type. Special care had been taken to minimize air resistance, and this resulted in no fender mirrors, a buried fuel filler, and an extremely small and narrow "Phantom" windshield (so called after the French fighting plane). On the Test Day at Le Mans, it was discovered that, owing to the long tail, exhaust gas infiltrated the cockpit. Accordingly, a megaphone muffler was hurriedly installed. Furthermore, in time for racing, a spoiler and vertical stabilizers were attached to the tail.

Thanks to its low air resistance, the 907 "Langheck" became Porsche's first car to break the 300 km/h barrier (186.4 mph). Given below is an interesting table comparing the maximum speeds of Porsche cars similarly fitted with a 6-cylinder, 2-liter engine.

906 Normal	165.9 mph
906 Long-tail ('66 Le Mans car)	171.4 mph
907 Long-tail	190.1 mph

When the 907 entered the '67 Le Mans to make its first campaign, public attention was focused on a decisive battle to be fought between the 7-liter Ford MK-4 and the 4-liter Ferrari P-4. Accordingly, Porsche entered the 910 and the 907 as well as the 906, modestly hoping for victory in the 2-liter class. The result was that the 907 placed fifth, the 910 sixth, and the 906 seventh and eighth. The ratios given below illustrate the high reliability of the Porsches.

	Cars entered	Cars finished
Porsche	6	4
Ford	9	2
Ferrari	7	2

Incidentally, the 907 was a right-hand drive type to suit racing on European circuits, which run clockwise and have many right turns.

907 "Langheck," which appeared for the first time on the Test Day at Le Mans in April, 1967

907 also on the Test Day at Le Mans

907 with which Elford/ Herrmann took fifth place overall and also won the Performance Index prize

Start of the 24-hour race at Daytona Beach

Short-tailed 907 that appeared in 1968

908

In 1968, FIA regulations were revised extensively, and Group-6 sports prototypes up to 3 liters and Group-4 (called Group-5 after 1970) sports cars up to 5-liters became able to compete together for the Manufacturer's Championship. As a result, Porsche, which had so far been obliged to compete, handicapped, against cars with greater engine displacement, such as the Ford and the Ferrari, could for the first time hope for overall victory.

Porsche's engineering staff then developed a completely new flat-8, 2,997-cc, 4-camshaft engine and mounted it in the 907 long-tail. This new machine, called the 908, was first sent to the Monza 1,000-km race. This new flat-8 engine was entirely different from the earlier 2,195-cc flat-8 (which was based on the Formula I engine of 1962). It was developed from the flat-6, 4-camshaft engine. The camshaft was driven by means of a long chain and gears attached to the end of the crankshaft, and was quite unlike the earlier flat-8, in which the camshaft was driven by means of a shaft and bevel gears. This new engine was a very powerful unit, having an output of 350 HP/8,400 rpm and a maximum torque of 235 lb.ft./6,600 rpm, and was provided with a 6-speed gearbox. The chassis and the body were practically the same as those of the 907 Longtail, the only difference being that the springs and shock absorbers had been strengthened. The wheel size, however, was changed from 13" to 15".

Special features of the 908 were the attachment of small vertical stabilizers to both sides of the tail and, behind them, an air spoiler was linked with the rear suspension. This latter mechanism was tested for the first time at Watkins Glen in the latter half of 1968. On the straightaway the spoiler was dipped at an angle of 35 degrees to develop a down thrust. The pair of flaps was linked by means of rods with the lower members of the suspension. When rolling

125

908 "Langheck"

occurred at a corner, the angle of the flap on the depressed side was decreased, resulting in a weaker aerodynamic down thrust. The other flap received greater air resistance thus reducing body roll and improving traction on the inside wheel. According to Elford, this action was effective at high-speed bends, but was practically ineffective at slow corners.

Following the 908 Long-tail there appeared at Nürburgring the 908, which had a 3-liter engine from the 907 Normal. The weight of the Long-tail type was 1,499 pounds and that of the Normal 1,455 pounds. The maximum speed of the Longtail was 198.8 mph, while that of the Normal was 183.3 mph. During that year, the new 908 was not yet powerful enough to be a main force in racing. Even though it won a victory at Nürburgring, it was inferior to the 907 in speed.

In 1969, when the FIA's regulations for Group 6 were extensively eased the 908 was changed into the Spyder, which was closer to a Group-7 car. Its chassis was not different from that of the coupé, but it had a 5-speed gearbox, and the car's weight was only 1,389 pounds (weight per horsepower: 3.9 lb/HP). Due to its higher air resistance, the maximum speed was 174 mph, but the 908 handled better, and was virtually unrivaled on medium-speed circuits. In early models, the light-alloy tubular frame had a tendency to crack. Accordingly, an inert gas was sealed, under pressure, in the frame tubes and a pressure gauge on the dashboard would warn the driver of a crack.

One may well say that the 908 held an unchallenged position during the 1969 season. Winning victories at Brands Hatch, Monza, Targa Florio, Spa, and Watkins Glen, it captured the coveted Manufacturers' Championship for Porsche.

Flat-8, 2,997-cc (79 x 60 mm), 4-camshaft engine newly developed for the 908

908 Normal coupé (top and bottom)

117

908 Spyder (top and bottom)

908 MK 3
Making its debut at the '70 Targa Florio, this car captured the first, second, fourth, and fifth places. It also won for Porsche consecutive victories for five years.

Rear end of the 908 MK 3

119

917

The crowing attraction of the Geneva Show held in March, 1969, was the Porsche 917 with a huge flat-12, 4.5-liter air-cooled engine. To Porsche it had been something of an obsession to reign supreme at Le Mans by defeating the 5-liter Ferrari 512 S and the Ford GT 40. The 917 was that very machine, and Porsche had secretly developed it for this purpose in the surprisingly short time of ten months. In order to obtain homologation for a Group-4 (now Group-5) sports car, Porsche manufactured 25 units of the 917 in a short period and marketed them at $35,000. The crankshaft of the huge flat-12, 4,494.2-cc (85 x 66 mm) engine was a 6-throw, 8-bearing type, and each of the crank journals was used jointly by two connecting rods (made of titanium alloy and weighing only 14.8 oz.). In order to prevent resonant vibrations, the long 12-cylinder engine crankshaft was divided at the middle into two parts. Camshaft and power take-off drives were both taken from this mid-point. The hemispherical combustion chamber and the valve angles were exactly the same as those of the 908.

Cooling was effected by means of a FRP fan, which was driven by the gear situated in the middle of the crankshaft. The fan had a speed of 7,400 rpm at an engine speed of 8,400 rpm and sent an air stream of 119.5 cu.ft/sec. with a power consumption of 17 HP. The engine output was 520 HP/8,000 rpm, with a torque of 332.7 lbs.ft./6,800 rpm.

The chassis of the 917 was identical to that of the 908, and its aluminium tube frame weighed only 103.6 pounds. As on the 908, the body was available in two types: Le Mans type Long-tail and Normal. According to Porsche, the maximum speeds of the two types were 236 mph and 211 mph, respectively. At various parts of the chassis, expensive alloys such as titanium and beryllium were used unsparingly. For example, the suspension springs and the steering rack and pinion were of titanium alloy, the brake discs were of beryllium alloy, and the hubs were of titanium alloy.

The 917, however, was not yet fully developed in 1969 for its debut season, and the reliability of its chassis was low. Complaints were heard that it was a very difficult car to drive. Its only victory was in Austria, in the final race of the season. In the 1970 season, Porsche itself stayed away from competition and entrusted its 917 cars to the J.W. Gulf team led by John Wyer and to Austria-Porsche. Porsche devoted its time to machine manufacture and support activities. In the meantime, the 917 finally reached maturity and began to display its capabilities to the fullest. Together with the 908, it captured the first three places at Le Mans and won for Porsche the Manufacturers' Championship for two consecutive years.

917 which was made public at the Geneva Show in March, 1969

134

917 "Langheck"

135

917's flat-12, DOHC, 4,494.2-cc, 520 HP engine snugly installed in the chassis

121

Structural drawing of the 917 "Kurz:" the short-tailed model of the 917, redesigned in 1970 according to John Wyer's practical advice

-BENNETT- M·SIA

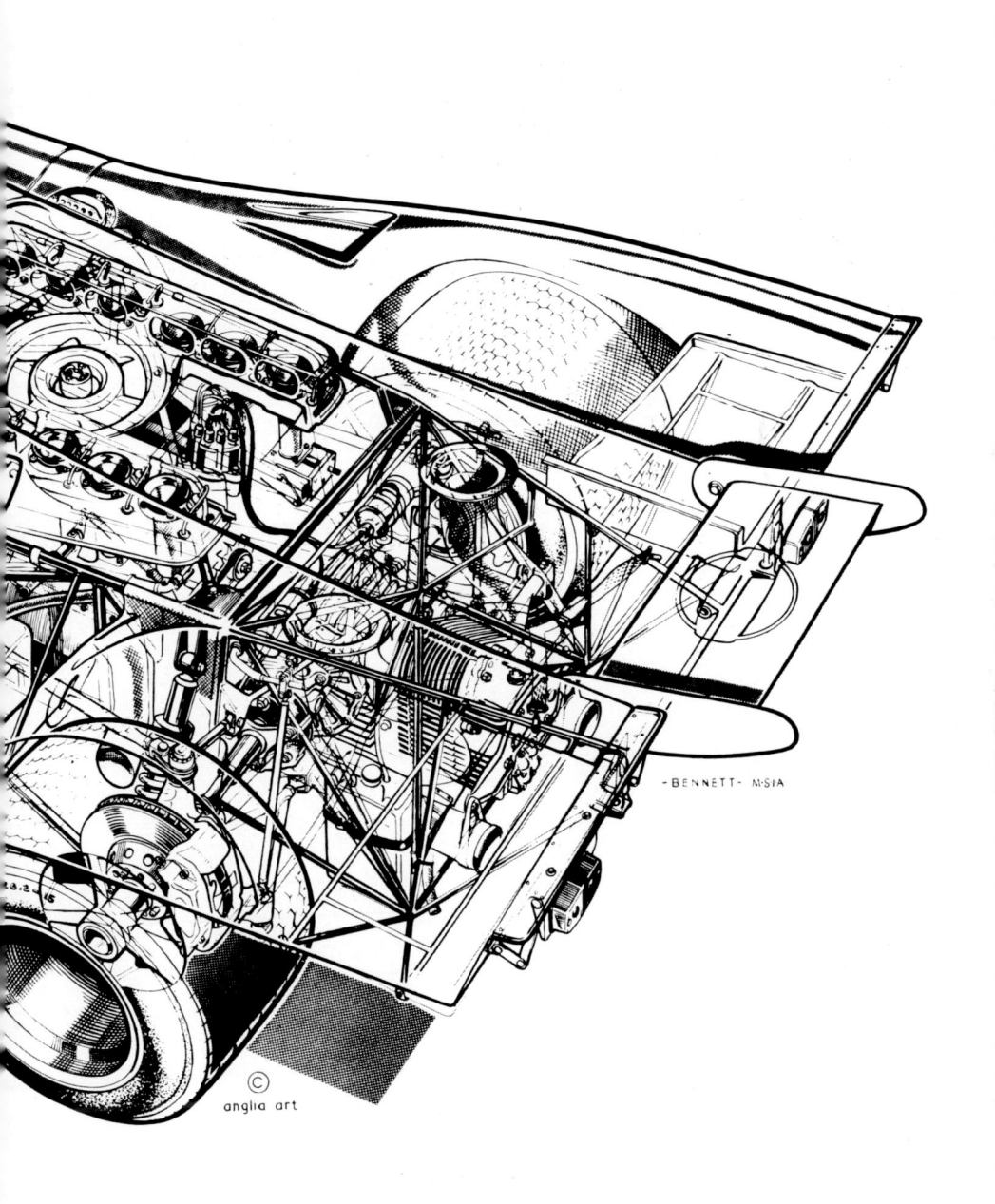

© anglia art

917 PA
This is the Group-7 version of the 917, which was entered by Porsche Audi (Porsche dealers in the U.S.A.) in the Can-Am series. In 1969, this car, driven by Jo Siffert, obtained the very good results of one third place, three fourth places, one fifth place, and one sixth place.

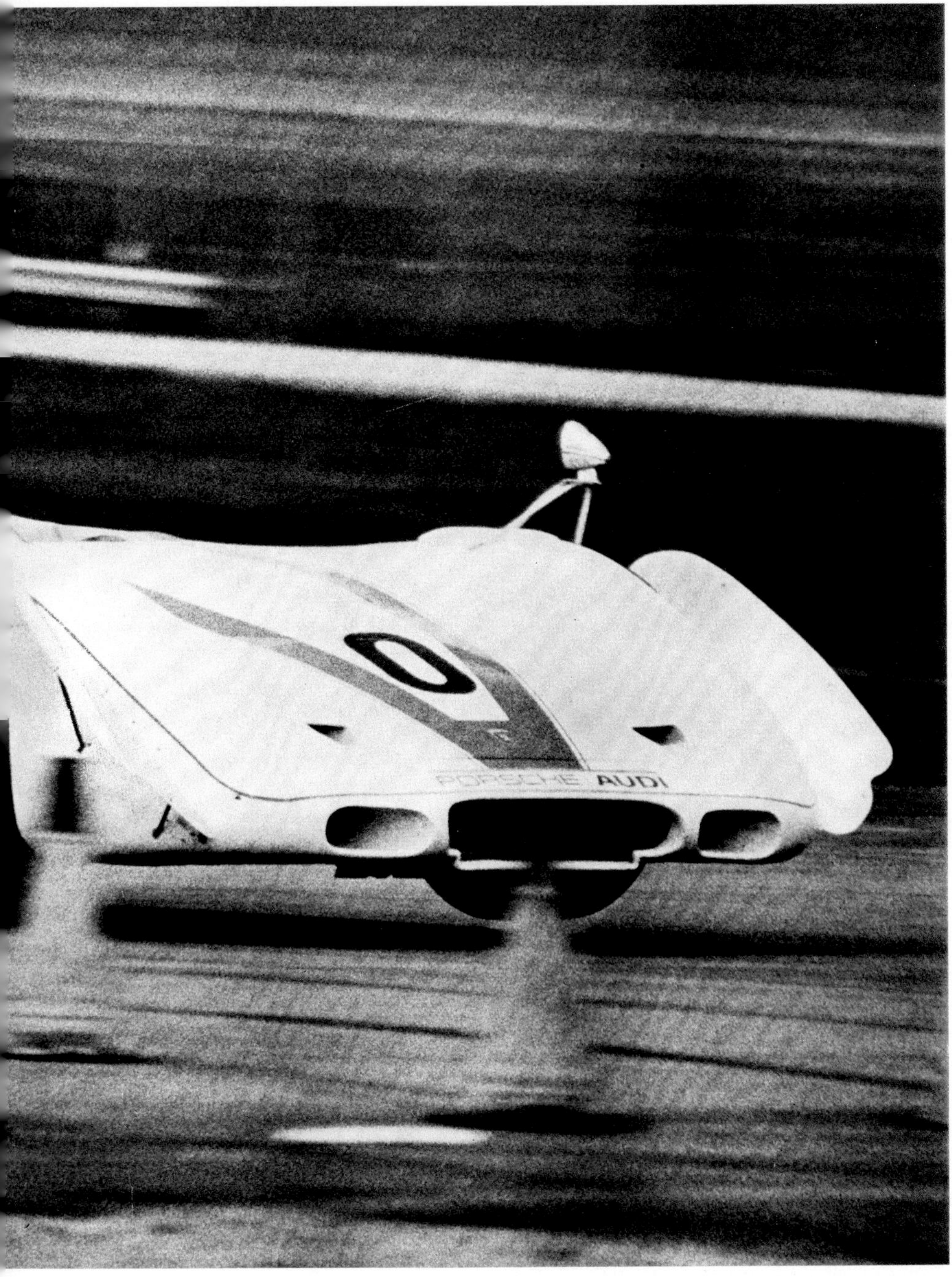
PORSCHE AUDI

Porsche Production Models (1950-1970)

year	type	cylinder valvegear	bore stroke (mm)	displacement (cc)	compression ratio	HP(DIN)	transmission	wheel base (in)	track (in)	overall length (in)	width (in)	height (in)	curb weight (DIN)
1950	356/1100	4 OHV	73.5×64	1086	7:1	40/4200	4+R	82.7	50.8/49.2	155.5*	65.4	51.2	1830
1951	356/1100	4 OHV	73.5×64	1086	7:1	40/4200	4+R	82.7	50.8/49.2	155.5*	65.4	51.2	1830
	356/1300	4 OHV	80×64	1286	6.5:1	44/4200	4+R	82.7	50.8/49.2	155.5*	65.4	51.2	1830
OCT.-	356/1500	4 OHV	80×74	1488	7:1	60/5000	4+R	82.7	50.8/49.2	155.5	65.4	51.2	1830
1952	356/1100	4 OHV	73.5×64	1086	7:1	40/4200	4+R	82.7	50.8/49.2	155.5	65.4	51.2	1830
	356/1300	4 OHV	80×64	1286	6.5:1	44/4200	4+R	82.7	50.8/49.2	155.5	65.4	51.2	1830
-SEP.	356/1500	4 OHV	80×74	1488	7:1	60/5000	4+R	82.7	50.8/49.2	155.5	65.4	51.2	1830
SEP.-	356/1500	4 OHV	80×74	1488	7:1	55/4400	4+R	82.7	50.8/49.2	155.5	65.4	51.2	1830
	356/1500S	4 OHV	80×74	1488	8.2:1	70/5000	4+R	82.7	50.8/49.2	155.5	65.4	51.2	1830
1953	356/1100	4 OHV	73.5×64	1086	7:1	40/4200	4+R	82.7	50.8/49.2	155.5	65.4	51.2	1830
	356/1300	4 OHV	80×64	1286	6.5:1	44/4200	4+R	82.7	50.8/49.2	155.5	65.4	51.2	1830
	356/1500	4 OHV	80×74	1488	7:1	55/4400	4+R	82.7	50.8/49.2	155.5	65.4	51.2	1830
	356/1500S	4 OHV	80×74	1488	8.2:1	70/5000	4+R	82.7	50.8/49.2	155.5	65.4	51.2	1830
NOV.-	356/1300S	4 OHV	74.5×74	1290	8.2:1	60/5500	4+R	82.7	50.8/49.2	155.5	65.4	51.2	1830
1954	356/1100	4 OHV	73.5×64	1086	7:1	40/4200	4+R	82.7	50.8/49.2	155.5	65.4	51.2	1830
	356/1300	4 OHV	80×64	1286	6.5:1	44/4200	4+R	82.7	50.8/49.2	155.5	65.4	51.2	1830
-MAY.	356/1300S	4 OHV	74.5×74	1290	8.2:1	60/5500	4+R	82.7	50.8/49.2	155.5	65.4	51.2	1830
JUN -NOV.	356/1300A	4 OHV	74.5×74	1290	6.5:1	44/4200	4+R	82.7	50.8/49.2	155.5	65.4	51.2	1830
-NOV.	356/1500	4 OHV	80×74	1488	7:1	55/4400	4+R	82.7	50.8/49.2	155.5	65.4	51.2	1830
	356/1500S	4 OHV	80×74	1488	8.2:1	70/5000	4+R	82.7	50.8/49.2	155.5	65.4	51.2	1830
	356/1300	4 OHV	74.5×74	1290	6.5:1	44/4200	4+R	82.7	50.8/49.2	155.5	65.4	51.2	1830
NOV.	356/1300S	4 OHV	74.5×74	1290	7.5:1	60/5500	4+R	82.7	50.8/49.2	155.5	65.4	51.2	1830
	356/1500	4 OHV	80×74	1488	7:1	55/4400	4+R	82.7	50.8/49.2	155.5	65.4	51.2	1830
	356/1500S	4 OHV	80×74	1488	8.2:1	70/5000	4+R	82.7	50.8/49.2	155.5	65.4	51.2	1830
1955	356/1300	4 OHV	74.5×74	1290	6.5:1	44/4200	4+R	82.7	50.8/49.2	155.5	65.4	51.2	1830
-OCT.	356/1300S	4 OHV	74.5×74	1290	7.5:1	60/5500	4+R	82.7	50.8/49.2	155.5	65.4	51.2	1830
	356/1500	4 OHV	80×74	1488	7:1	55/4400	4+R	82.7	50.8/49.2	155.5	65.4	51.2	1830
	356/1500S	4 OHV	80×74	1488	8.2:1	70/5000	4+R	82.7	50.8/49.2	155.5	65.4	51.2	1830
	356A/1300	4 OHV	74.5×74	1290	6.5:1	44/4200	4+R	82.7	51.4/50.1	155.5*	65.8	51.6	1874
	356A/1300S	4 OHV	74.5×74	1290	7.5:1	60/5500	4+R	82.7	51.4/50.1	155.5	65.8	51.6	1874
OCT.-	356A/1600	4 OHV	82.5×74	1582	7.5:1	60/4500	4+R	82.7	51.4/50.1	155.5	65.8	51.6	1874
	356A/1600S	4 OHV	82.5×74	1582	8.5:1	75/5000	4+R	82.7	51.4/50.1	155.5	65.8	51.6	1874
1956	356A/1300	4 OHV	74.5×74	1290	6.5:1	44/4200	4+R	82.7	51.4/50.1	155.5	65.8	51.6	1874
	356A/1300S	4 OHV	74.5×74	1290	7.5:1	60/5500	4+R	82.7	51.4/50.1	155.5	65.8	51.6	1874
	356A/1600	4 OHV	82.5×74	1582	7.5:1	60/4500	4+R	82.7	51.4/50.1	155.5	65.8	51.6	1874
	356A/1600S	4 OHV	82.5×74	1582	8.5:1	75/5000	4+R	82.7	51.4/50.1	155.5	65.8	51.6	1874
1957	356A/1300S	4 OHV	74.5×74	1290	6.5:1	44/4200	4+R	82.7	51.4/50.1	155.5	65.8	51.6	1874
	356A/1300S	4 OHV	74.5×74	1290	7.5:1	60/5500	4+R	82.7	51.4/50.1	155.5	65.8	51.6	1874

year	type	cylinder valvegear	bore stroke (mm)	displacement (cc)	compression ratio	H.P.(DIN)	transmission	wheel base (in)	track (in)	overall length (in)	width (in)	height (in)	curb weight (DIN)
1957	356A/1600	4 OHV	82.5×74	1582	7.5 : 1	60/4500	4 + R	82.7	51.4/50.1	155.5	65.8	51.6	1874
	356A/1600S	4 OHV	82.5×74	1582	8.5 : 1	75/5000	4 + R	82.7	51.4/50.1	155.5	65.8	51.6	1874
1958 SEP.	356A/1600	4 OHV	82.5×74	1582	7.5 : 1	60/4500	4 + R	82.7	51.4/50.1	155.5	65.8	51.6	1874
	356A/1600S	4 OHV	82.5×74	1582	8.5 : 1	75/5000	4 + R	82.7	51.4/50.1	155.5	65.8	51.6	1874
1959	356B/1600	4 OHV	82.5×74	1582	7.5 : 1	60/4500	4 + R	82.7	51.4/50.1	157.9‡	65.8	52.4	1984
	356B/1600S	4 OHV	82.5×74	1582	8.5 : 1	75/5000	4 + R	82.7	51.4/50.1	157.9	65.8	52.4	1984
1960	356B/1600	4 OHV	82.5×74	1582	7.5 : 1	60/4500	4 + R	82.7	51.4/50.1	157.9	65.8	52.4	1984
	356B/1600S	4 OHV	82.5×74	1582	8.5 : 1	75/5000	4 + R	82.7	51.4/50.1	157.9	65.8	52.4	1984
	356B/1600-S90	4 OHV	82.5×74	1582	9 : 1	90/5500	4 + R	82.7	51.4/50.1	157.9	65.8	52.4	1984
1961	356B/1600	4 OHV	82.5×74	1582	7.5 : 1	60/4500	4 + R	82.7	51.4/50.1	157.9	65.8	52.4	1984
	356B/1600S	4 OHV	82.5×74	1582	8.5 : 1	75/5000	4 + R	82.7	51.4/50.1	157.9	65.8	52.4	1984
	356B/1600-S90	4 OHV	82.5×74	1582	9 : 1	90/5500	4 + R	82.7	51.4/50.1	157.9	65.8	52.4	1984
1962	356B/1600	4 OHV	82.5×74	1582	7.5 : 1	60/4500	4 + R	82.7	51.4/50.1	157.9	65.8	52.4	1984
	356B/1600S	4 OHV	82.5×74	1582	8.5 : 1	75/5000	4 + R	82.7	51.4/50.1	157.9	65.8	52.4	1984
	356B/1600-S90	4 OHV	82.5×74	1582	9 : 1	90/5500	4 + R	82.7	51.4/50.1	157.9	65.8	52.4	1984
1963 JUL.-	356C/1600C	4 OHV	82.5×74	1582	8.5 : 1	75/5200	4 + R	82.7	51.4/50.1	157.9	65.8	51.8	2061
	356C/1600SC	4 OHV	82.5×74	1582	9.5 : 1	95/5800	4 + R	82.7	51.4/50.1	157.9	65.8	51.8	2061
1964 JUL.-	356C/1600C	4 OHV	82.5×74	1582	8.5 : 1	75/5200	4 + R	82.7	51.4/50.1	157.9	65.8	51.8	2061
	356C/1600SC	4 OHV	82.5×74	1582	9.5 : 1	95/5800	4 + R	82.7	51.4/50.1	157.9	65.8	51.8	2061
	911 deluxe	6 SOHC	66×80	1991	9 : 1	130/6100	5 + R	87.0	53.8/52.8	163.9	63.4	52.0	2381
1965 MAY.-	911 deluxe	6 SOHC	80×66	1991	9 : 1	130/6100	5 + R	87.0	53.8/52.8	163.9	63.4	52.0	2381
	912	4 OHV	82.5×74	1582	9.3 : 1	90/5800	5 + R	87.0	53.8/52.6	163.9	63.4	52.0	2138
1966 SEP.-	911N	6 SOHC	80×66	1991	9 : 1	130/6100	5 + R	87.0	53.8/52.8	163.9	63.4	52.0	2381
	911S	6 SOHC	80×66	1991	9.8 : 1	160/6600	5 + R	87.0	53.8/52.6	163.9	63.4	52.0	2271
1967 SEP.-	911S	6 SOHC	80×66	1991	9.8 : 1	160/6600	5 + R	87.0	53.8/52.8	163.9	63.4	52.0	2271
	911L	6 SOHC	80×66	1991	9 : 1	130/6100	5 + R	87.0	53.8/52.8	163.9	63.4	52.0	2381
	911T	6 SOHC	80×66	1991	8.6 : 1	110/5800	5 + R	87.0	53.8/52.8	163.9	63.4	52.0	2271
1968	911S	6 SOHC	80×66	1991	9.9 : 1	170/6800	5 + R	89.4	54.1/53.3	163.9	63.4	52.0	2194
	911E	6 SOHC	80×66	1991	9.1 : 1	140/6500	5 + R	89.4	54.1/53.3	163.9	63.4	52.0	2249
	911T	6 SOHC	80×66	1991	8.6 : 1	110/5800	5 + R	89.4	53.5/53.0	163.9	63.4	52.0	2249
1969	911S	6 SOHC	84×66	2195	9.8 : 1	180/6500	5 + R	89.4	53.5/53.0	163.9	63.4	52.0	2194
	911E	6 SOHC	84×66	2195	9.1 : 1	155/6200	5 + R	89.4	53.5/53.0	163.9	63.4	52.0	2249
	911T	6 SOHC	84×66	2195	8.6 : 1	125/5800	5 + R	89.4	53.5/53.0	163.9	63.4	52.0	2249
	914	4 OHV	90×66	1679	8.2 : 1	80/4900	5 + R	96.5	52.6/54.1	156.9	65.0	48.0	1984
	914/6	6 SOHC	80×66	1991	8.6 : 1	110/5800	5 + R	96.5	53.6/54.4	156.9	65.0	48.4	2072

* coupé cabriolet ‡ coupé hardtop

Credits

Die ungewöhnliche Geschichte des Hauses Porsche: Richard von Frankenberg, Motor-Presse Verlag GmbH., Stuttgart.

Beyond Expectation: K. B. Hopfinger, G. T. Foulis & Co., Ltd., London.

Porsche: Anthony Pritchard, Pelham Books Ltd., London.

The Porsche and VW Companion: Kenneth Ullyett. Stanley Paul & Co., Ltd., London.

Porsche Story: Julius Weitmann. ARCO Publishing Co., Inc., New York.

German High-performance Cars 1894-1965: Jerrold Sloniger & Hans-Heinrich von Fersen. B. T. Batsford Ltd., London.

Christophorus: Porsche house magazine.